INFORMATION TECHNOLOGY
A Revolutionary Change

INFORMATION TECHNOLOGY
A Revolutionary Change
(In 9 Volumes)

Volume 5
(Net Based Guidance and Councelling)

Editor
RAMESH CHANDRA
Vice-Chancellor, Bundelkhand University, Jhansi (U.P.)

KALPAZ PUBLICATIONS
DELHI–110052

INFORMATION TECHNOLOGY: A REVOLUTIONARY CHANGE
(Information Technology)

Rs. 8000 (Set)
Rs. 900 (Each Volume)

ISBN: 81-7835-201-X (Set)
ISBN: 81-7835-224-9 (Vol. 5)

Published in 2003 in India by
Kalpaz Publications
C–30, Satyawati Nagar
Delhi–110052
E-mail: kalpaz@hotmail.com

Laser Typesetting at: Varsha Graphics, Delhi
Printed at: Mehra Offset Printers, New Delhi

Contents

Preface

We are living in an information age and advanced technology continues to influence the lives in the world of work and at home. Computers, the World Wide Web, the Internet, and e-mail are discussed on a regular basis. The Internet is quickly becoming a revolutionary force in everyday private and business life. Many of the interest assessment devices and occupational data bases available via computer based systems are now available online via the Internet. Thus, the benefits and possible drawbacks of providing this information via computer apply to the provision of this information via the Internet.

Net-based guidance and counselling programmes involve synchronous distance interaction among counsellors and clients using what is seen and heard via video to communicate. The standards which govern the practice of Internet counselling are intended for use by counsellors, clients, the public, counsellor educators, and organizations that examine and deliver Internet counselling. These standards are intended to address practices that are unique to Internet counselling and Internet counsellors and do not duplicate principles found in traditional codes of ethics.

Within the limits of readily available technology, Internet counsellors have an obligation to make their

Web site a barrier-free environment to clients with disabilities. Internet counsellors are aware that some clients may communicate in different languages, live in different time zones, and have unique cultural perspectives. Internet counsellors are also aware that local conditions and events may impact the client. The rapid development and use of the Internet to deliver information and foster communication has resulted in the creation of new forms of counselling. Developments have occurred so rapidly that it is difficult to communicate a common understanding of these new forms of counselling practice.

Counsellors need to become electronically and technologically competent to appreciate career development, job hunting, and employment difficulties in the twenty-first century. However, it is warned that technology cannot replace basic career counselling skills for a number of reasons. Acknowledging the impact of technology on guidance and counselling, internet resources are provided for use by counselling professionals and clients in conjunction with professionals.

The main controversies regarding the use of technology in counselling involves the use of computers to provide career guidance counselling and the use of the Internet in career counselling. Underlying these controversies, however, is a more fundamental issue, the purpose of guidance and counselling The counselling and guidance profession has seemingly indicated its acceptance of this use of computer technology within career counselling, as many colleges and universities and government centers now use career information delivery systems.

Editor

1

Internet-based Counselling

Counseling is the application of mental health, psychological, or human development principles, through cognitive, affective, behavioral or systemic intervention strategies, that address wellness, personal growth, or career development, as well as pathology. Depending on the needs of the client and the availability of services, counseling may range from a few brief interactions in a short period of time, to numerous interactions over an extended period of time. Brief interventions, such as classroom discussions, workshop presentations, or assistance in using assessment, information, or instructional resources, may be sufficient to meet individual needs. Or, these brief interventions may lead to longer-term counseling interventions for individuals with more substantial needs. Counseling may be delivered by a single counselor, two counselors working collaboratively, or a single counselor with brief assistance from another counselor who has specialized expertise that is needed by the client.

Forms of counseling differ with respect to participants, delivery location, communication medium, and interaction process. Counseling participants can be individuals, couples, or groups. The location for counseling delivery can be face-to-face or at a distance with the assistance of technology. The communication medium for counseling can be what is read from text, what is heard from audio, or what is seen and heard in person or from video. The interaction process for counseling can be synchronous or asynchronous. Synchronous interaction occurs with little or no gap in time between the responses of the counselor and the client. Asynchronous interaction occurs with a gap in time between the responses of the counselor and the client.

The selection of a specific form of counseling is based on the needs and preferences of the client within the range of services available. Distance counseling supplements face-to-face counseling by providing increased access to counseling on the basis of necessity or convenience. Barriers, such as being a long distance from counseling services, geographic separation of a couple, or limited physical mobility as a result of having a disability, can make it necessary to provide counseling at a distance. Options, such as scheduling counseling sessions outside of traditional service delivery hours or delivering counseling services at a place of residence or employment, can make it more convenient to provide counseling at a distance.

A taxonomy of currently available forms of counseling practice are given below:

— Face-To-Face Counseling

— Individual Counseling

— Couple Counseling

— Group Counseling

— Technology-Assisted Distance Counseling

— Telecounseling

— Telephone-Based Individual Counseling

— Telephone-Based Couple Counseling

— Telephone-Based Group Counseling

— Internet Counseling

— E-Mail-Based Individual Counseling

— Chat-Based Individual Counseling —

— Chat-Based Couple Counseling

— Chat-Based Group Counseling

— Video-Based Individual Counseling

— Video-Based Couple Counseling

— Video-Based Group Counseling

Face-to-face counseling for individuals, couples, and groups involves synchronous interaction between and among counselors and clients using what is seen and heard in person to communicate.

Technology-assisted distance counseling for individuals, couples, and groups involves the use of the telephone or the computer to enable counselors and clients to communicate at a distance when circumstances make this approach necessary or convenient.

Telecounseling involves synchronous distance interaction among counselors and clients using one-to-one or conferencing features of the telephone to communicate.

Telephone-based individual counseling involves synchronous distance interaction between a counselor and a client using what is heard via audio to communicate.

Telephone-based couple counseling involves synchronous distance interaction among a counselor or counselors and a couple using what is heard via audio to communicate.

Telephone-based group counseling involves synchronous distance interaction among counselors and clients using what is heard via audio to communicate. Internet counseling involves asynchronous and synchronous distance interaction among counselors and clients using e-mail, chat, and videoconferencing features of the Internet to communicate.

E-mail-based individual Internet counseling involves asynchronous distance interaction between counselor and client using what is read via text to communicate.

Chat-based individual Internet counseling involves synchronous distance interaction between counselor and client using what is read via text to communicate.

Chat-based couple Internet counseling involves synchronous distance interaction among a counselor or counselors and a couple using what is read via text to communicate.

Chat-based group Internet counseling involves synchronous distance interaction among counselors and clients using what is read via text to communicate.

Video-based individual Internet counseling involves synchronous distance interaction between counselor and client using what is seen and heard via video to communicate.

Video-based couple Internet counseling involves synchronous distance interaction among a counselor or counselors and a couple using what is seen and heard via video to communicate.

Video-based group Internet counseling involves synchronous distance interaction among counselors and clients using what is seen and heard via video to communicate.

The standards which govern the practice of Internet counseling are intended for use by counselors, clients, the public, counselor educators, and organizations that examine and deliver Internet counseling. These standards are intended to address practices that are unique to Internet counseling and Internet counselors and do not duplicate principles found in traditional codes of ethics.

Internet counseling standards of practice are based upon the principles of ethical practice embodied in the NBCC Code of Ethics. Therefore, these standards should be used in conjunction with the most recent version of the NBCC ethical code. Related content in the NBCC Code are indicated in parentheses after each standard. Recognizing that significant new technology emerges continuously, these standards should be reviewed frequently. It is also recognized that Internet counseling ethics cases should be reviewed in light of delivery systems existing at the moment rather than at the time the standards were adopted.

In situations where it is difficult to verify the identity of the Internet client, steps are taken to address impostor concerns, such as by using code words or numbers. Internet counselors determine if a client is a minor and therefore in need of parental/guardian consent. When parent/guardian consent is required to provide Internet counseling to minors, the identity of the consenting person is verified.

As part of the counseling orientation process, the Internet counselor explains to clients the procedures for contacting the Internet counselor when he or she is off-line and, in the case of asynchronous counseling, how often e-mail messages will be checked by the Internet counselor.

As part of the counseling orientation process, the Internet counselor explains to clients the possibility of technology failure and discusses alternative modes of communication, if that failure occurs.

As part of the counseling orientation process, the Internet counselor explains to clients how to cope with potential misunderstandings when visual cues do not exist.

As a part of the counseling orientation process, the Internet counselor collaborates with the Internet client to identify an appropriately trained professional who can provide local assistance, including crisis intervention, if needed.

The Internet counselor and Internet client should also collaborate to determine the local crisis hotline telephone number and the local emergency telephone number. The Internet counselor has an obligation, when appropriate, to make clients aware of free public access points to the Internet within the community for accessing Internet counseling or Web-based assessment, information, and instructional resources.

Within the limits of readily available technology, Internet counselors have an obligation to make their Web site a barrier-free environment to clients with disabilities. Internet counselors are aware that some clients may communicate in different languages, live in different time zones, and have unique cultural perspectives. Internet counselors are also aware that local conditions and events may impact the client.

The rapid development and use of the Internet to deliver information and foster communication has resulted in the creation of new forms of counseling. Developments have occurred so rapidly that it is difficult to communicate a common understanding of these new forms of counseling practice.

The Internet counselor informs Internet clients of encryption methods being used to help insure the security of client/counselor/supervisor communications.

Encryption methods should be used whenever possible. If encryption is not made available to clients, clients must be informed of the potential hazards of unsecured communication on the Internet. Hazards may include unauthorized monitoring of transmissions and/or records of Internet counseling sessions.

The Internet counselor informs Internet clients if, how, and how long session data are being preserved.

Session data may include Internet counselor/Internet client e-mail, test results, audio/video session recordings, session notes, and counselor/supervisor communications. The likelihood of electronic sessions being preserved is greater because of the ease and decreased costs involved in recording. Thus, its potential use in supervision, research, and legal proceedings increases.

Internet counselors follow appropriate procedures regarding the release of information for sharing Internet client information with other electronic sources. Because of the relative ease with which e-mail messages can be forwarded to formal and casual referral sources, Internet counselors must work to insure the confidentiality of the Internet counseling relationship.

Internet counselors review pertinent legal and ethical codes for guidance on the practice of Internet counseling and supervision. Local, state, provincial, and national statutes as well as codes of professional membership organizations, professional certifying bodies, and state or provincial licensing boards need to be reviewed. Also, as varying state rules and opinions exist on questions pertaining to whether Internet counseling takes place in the Internet counselor's location or the Internet client's location, it is important to review codes in the counselor's home jurisdiction as well as the client's. Internet counselors also consider carefully local customs regarding age of consent and child abuse reporting, and liability insurance policies need to be reviewed to determine if the practice of Internet counseling is a covered activity.

Computer-related Technology in Counseling

During the past 30 years, counseling professionals have shifted their focus on the application of computer-related technology (CRT) to counseling tasks that center on therapeutic intervention and counselor supervision. Particular attention has been given to positive and negative aspects of using the Internet as a medium for service delivery. Although counseling via the Internet, typically referred to as "cybercounseling" or "webtherapy", has received so much attention lately, there has been scant exploration of

(1) the extent to which counselors are using various other types of CRT in their work, and

(2) other work-related tasks performed by counselors that could be aided by CRT.

Cybercounseling is not the only way counselors can use the Internet in their practice. Likewise, although therapeutic intervention may be the focal task that counselors perform in their work, CRT can help counselors perform many other work-related tasks included in marketing, record-keeping, and professional development. The potential uses for Internet-based CRT tools by counselors to accomplish specific work-related tasks include:

Internet-based CRT Tools	*Potential Uses by Counselors*
1. electronic mail (e-mail)	therapy; marketing; screening; client/therapistcorrespondences for scheduling, inter-session monitoring and posttherapeutic follow-up; client record trans-fer; referrals; intake; homework and professional collegiality
2. websites/homepages	marketing/advertising; information dissemination; and publications
3. videoconferencing	therapy; homework; referrals; and consultation
4. bulletin board systems	consultation; referrals; resou-rces for information; and professional collegiality
5. computerized simulation	supervision and skills training
6. databases/FTP sites	research; information resources for therapists; self-help librar-ies; client record transfers; and assessment and analyses
7. chats/electronic discussion	group therapy; self-help; and support
8. software	skills training; self-help; and homework.

There are other, non-Internet-based CRT tools that counseling professionals may find valuable in their work:

Non-Internetbased CRT Tools	*Potential Uses by Counselors*
1. spreadsheets	record keeping; data organization; client information; and research
2. word processors	record keeping; correspondence; marketing; and research publication
3. software	skills training for the professional and clients; self-help information; marketing; office management; reference sources; and case-notes

Use of computer applications by counseling professionals has continued to steadily increase with a particularly rapid expansion of computer use in the early 1980's. In these pioneering years of CRT use, counseling professionals concentrated primarily on the development of software programs designed to simulate therapists, computer-assisted career guidance systems, and computer-assisted testing and assessment

A great deal of technology is available for use by mental health professionals in a variety of work-related tasks. To date, no trend assessment has been made concerning the variety of ways CRT might be used by mental health counselors and counselor educators to perform all aspects of their work, including therapeutic intervention and supervision, in the near future. Without these assessments, educators and policy makers lack important information that could enable them to better design training programs for preparing professionals to upgrade their skills in order to remain competitive in a field struggling for independent identity. These assessments would also help establish long overdue computer competency requirements and training standards for the next generation of counselors to meet the demands of a technologically sophisticated clientele. Information concerning the extent and types of CRT use by counselors both now and in the next 10 years could also provide a foundation to help guide research into many of the issues raised by an ever-increasing use of the Internet as a vehicle for counseling service delivery.

In order to ensure competent and standardized acquisition of the technological skills important to the work of counseling professionals, both now and in the future, counselor training programs must adopt mandatory evaluation of continuously updated minimal computer skills. By so doing, professional counselors and counselor educators will be in a better position to take advantage of the opportunities offered by new technologies, to remain professionally competitive in an increasingly technological world, and begin meaningful research to proactively guide technology's development and use by mental health professionals.

Delphi method

Delphi is a method of acquiring the opinions of a group of geographically dispersed individuals, considered experts in their occupational fields, who remain anonymous to each other throughout the data-gathering process. The group of experts is referred to as the Delphi panel. Panel members are sent a series of questionnaires, called rounds, which list a number of statements pertinent to the topic of investigation. Statements are to be rated by the experts, and returned to the investigator for summarization. After each round of questions, summary data, in the form of a median or mean response for each statement, are computed by the investigator, and relayed to the panel of experts in the subsequent round of questions. Panelists are then asked to consider the summary responses of other members, give a new response to each statement, and provide reasons for non-compliance with the group rating. This process continues until group consensus is reached or as dictated by the researcher. After the last round of questions are returned and analyzed, panelists are provided the final summary results of their ratings.

There are many variations on the traditional Delphi first developed in the 1950's for the RAND Corporation by Olaf Helmer and Norman Dalkey. In a standard Delphi, the initial round of questions sent to the panel of experts are open-ended, allowing panel members the freedom to provide information that the investigator will use to create the Delphi questionnaire. In a modified Delphi, this phase of the Delphi process may be completed by a committee of individuals representative of the Delphi panel prior to the beginning of the rounds of questioning. A futures Delphi asks panelists for their opinions on matters that may occur in a future time frame.

Nominations for the Delphi experts were acquired through a search of major publications in the fields of counseling and computer technology, posting formal requests to professional listservs on the Internet, requests made to departmental chairpersons at major U.S. universities, and by personal referrals. Correspondences with Delphi panel members were conducted via e-mail.

In a study counselor and technologist nominees were asked to have achieved the following description of expert status:

An expert may be defined as someone with special skills or knowledge evidenced by leadership in professional organizations, holding office in professional organizations, presenter at national conventions, published in recognized journals, etc.

Additionally, counselor nominees were asked to meet the requirements for and hold the title of National Certified Counselor and/or Licensed Professional Counselor in their state of practice or to have held such titles, and to have counseled individuals on issues of mental health for a period of at least five years. Counselor nominees were required to possess expertise in at least one of the following four counselor categories:

— Counselor educators defined as persons currently employed by an accredited college or university to instruct master's and/or doctoral-level students in counseling.

— Counselors who work in agency settings such as state mental hospitals, community mental health agencies, or large, corporate-owned mental health agencies.

— Counselors who work in private practice, either as an individual or with other individuals.

— Counselors who work in college or university counseling centers that help students with a variety of mental health issues.

In addition to having achieved the above description of expert status, technologist nominees were asked to possess demonstrated skills and/or titles in computer-related technology including, but not limited to:

designing and/or developing web pages; computer programming; software development; knowledge of operating systems; network administrator; hold a computer science degree; background in engineering; instructional technologist; information systems manager; and/or database administrator.

Delphi panel of the study was consisted of 5 counselor educators, 7 private practitioners, 3 agency counselors, 8 counselors who work in university counseling centers, and 7 computer-related technologists, for a total of 30 panelists completing the Delphi Round 1 questionnaire.

Questionnaires were developed for the Delphi study by committee members representative of the Delphi panelists, and posted in a web-accessible database by the study's computer programmer. In an effort to achieve a more accurate understanding of the opinions expressed by the Delphi panelists, the research questions for the study were posed from several perspectives.

The Round 1 questionnaire asked panelists to rate 46 generic counselor tasks in 7 task categories for current and future use of CRT, and to provide specific examples of current and future CRT use in counseling.

The Round 2 questionnaire asked panelists to rate 7 new counselor tasks, including 1 new category of tasks, provided by them during Round 1, and to indicate frequency of use for 10 specific CRT tools.

The Round 3 questionnaire listed all 53 counselor tasks in 8 categories of tasks. Panel members were asked to review their previous ratings of each task in consideration of group median ratings and make final ratings for how much counselors and counselor educators use CRT to accomplish the work-related tasks, both now and for the year 2008. Finally, panelists were requested to select reasons for their final ratings of CRT use and non-use. It was during Round 3 that individual members of the Delphi panel of experts, after consideration of the median responses of other panel members, gave their final ratings of the completed list of 53 counselor tasks in 8 categories for use of CRT to complete those tasks, both now and in 2008. Each task was rated twice-once for current and once for future use of CRT-using the following scale:

— 5 = Essential if it allows counselors to do things they never could do before

— 4 = Very Helpful if it significantly decreases effort, make things much more efficient, or improves the quality of the product or service

— 3 = Helpful if it makes the job easier to perform, but is not essential

— 2 = Not used, but would like to if CRT and/or the skills to use it are not currently available, but would be used if they were available

— 1 = Not used, and no need for if there is no interest in using CRT for the task, its use would be inappropriate for the task, or no desire to use.

Panel responses to the final Delphi Round 3 questionnaire task ratings were summarized using eight steps. Results indicating counselor tasks accomplished with the help of CRT, both currently and for the year 2008. Tasks panel members rated as "2" for both time frames. In Round 2, Part B, counselor panelists were asked to indicate how often they, personally, used the following 10 specific CRT tools for each of 7 counselor task categories by choosing "NA" for Not Applicable, "D" for Daily use, "W" for Weekly use, "O" for Occasional use, or "N" for Never use: e-mail, word processor, web, spread sheet, project management, graphics, animation, simulation, statistics software, or other.

Technologist panel members were asked to indicate how often they felt counseling professionals were using each of the 10 CRT tools. Panel responses to the Delphi Round 2 questionnaire CRT tool usage ratings were summarized using four steps. Results of Round 2 CRT tool usage ratings, grouped by CRT tool item. Round 2 CRT tool usage ratings, grouped by counselor task category. After Delphi panelists had given their Round 3 final rating of each counselor task for both current and future use of CRT, they were asked to indicate the following reasons for their final choices: E = Efficiency means able to produce more with less effort, Q = Quality means able to produce a superior product or service; can do the job, and O = Opportunity means able to do things that may not have been previously possible, as reasons for using CRT. For tasks for which CRT was not used, panelists were asked to indicated the following reasons: T = lack of Training to use, C = Costs of soft/hardware, S = no available Software, I = CRT is Inappropriate to task, or O = Other, please write in and reasons for not using CRT.

The Delphi study addressed four research questions. Major findings are summarized below:

Research question 1: How much do counselors and counselor educators rely on computer-related technology to complete job-related tasks today?

Answer: It has been proposed that CRT can be used to assist counseling professionals in numerous ways. The data from the study suggest counselors and counselor educators are using CRT to assist them in over half (59%) of job-related tasks today. The experts in this Delphi inquiry indicated that counselors currently find CRT helpful in making 40% of generic work-related tasks (31 of 53 tasks) easier to accomplish, e.g., professional writing, preparation and delivery of advertising, and test administration and scoring. In addition, the experts believe CRT to be very helpful in significantly decreasing effort, increasing efficiency, or improving the quality or services of another 19% (10 of 53) of work-related activities. In all, the experts indicated that counselors and counselor educators currently rely on CRT to complete 59% of job-related tasks. In addition, counselor experts who participated in the study reported at least weekly use of a variety of CRT tools in their work.

Research question 2: Which counselor-related tasks are counseling professionals currently accomplishing with the help of CRT?

Answer: All categories of work-related tasks are represented in current CRT use assessment with the exception of tasks concerning professional accountability. The experts in the Delphi study rated CRT use as helpful for: all counselor tasks listed related to marketing/client recruitment, report and record-keeping (paperwork), clinical assessment/testing, and consultation and referral; all but one task in supervision/training; and all but two tasks in professional development. Half (50-57%) of the counselor experts expressed the opinion that CRT is not currently being utilized by professional counselors for most therapeutic intervention tasks, such as establishing rapport with clients, confidentiality discussions, evaluating presenting problems, and utilizing affective interventions, because CRT is inappropriate for these tasks. In addition, these experts indicated therapeutic tasks involving the determination of treatment length and interventions using cognitive, behavioral, or a combination of therapeutic techniques were not currently being accomplished with the help of CRT due to a lack of available software.

In all, only 3 of 18 in-session intervention/therapy/counseling tasks and no tasks in professional accountability were thought to be currently accomplished with use of CRT. However, the panel of experts suggested counselors would like to use CRT for these tasks if the technology or skills were available.

Research question 3: What are specific ways in which counselors and counselor educators are currently using CRT in performing job-related tasks?

Answer: Various CRT tools have been explored in the literature as potentially useful to mental health professionals in their work. Results of the Delphi study indicate counselors and counselor educators are utilizing a large variety of CRT tools in their work. Delphi panelists gave 73 specific examples of current CRT use by counselors and counselor educators for work-related activities. These examples fell into three main categories. The first category included the use of software for word processing, spreadsheets, statistical analysis, and publishing for tasks in marketing/client-recruitment, report and record-keeping, insession intervention/therapy/counseling, clinical assessment/testing, and professional development. The second category of examples included use of e-mail, both private and on professional listservs, for activities in therapy, consultation and referral, super-vision/training, and professional development. The third category of CRT examples involved use of the WWW, including websites, chat-rooms, and teleconferencing, for tasks in marketing, therapy, consultation and referral, super-vision/training, and professional development. Panelists expressed caution about current CRT security issues where client data is concerned.

Research question 4: How much and in what ways will CRT be used by counselors and counselor educators to do their work in the next ten years?

Answer: The experts in the study forecast a significant increase in use of CRT by professional counselors in the near future. It is expected that counselors will be utilizing CRT for at least 90% of their work, in all categorical aspects, including professional accountability. The Delphi experts indicated they believe counselors will find CRT very helpful in significantly decreasing effort, increasing efficiency, or improving the quality of services for 72% (38 of 53) of counselor tasks by the year 2008. CRT will be helpful in making the job easier to perform for another 21% (11 of 53) of work-related tasks. In all, counselor and technologist panel members agreed that 92% of the work counselors do in 2008, including all task categories, i.e., marketing/client recruitment, report and record-keeping (paperwork), in-session intervention/therapy/counseling, clinical assessment/testing, consultation and referral, supervision/training, professional development, and professional accountability, and all but 4 individual generic tasks, will be accomplished with the help of CRT. Three of the tasks for which panelists believe CRT will not be used were therapeutic activities, while the fourth concerned professional accountability. However, experts in the study suggested that if the technology or skills were available in 2008, counselors would use CRT to accomplish these tasks as well. The only reason given by half of the counselor experts for not using CRT in 2008 was that CRT is inappropriate for the specific task of confidentiality discussions with clients.

Finally, panelists gave 79 specific examples of how they believe counselors will use CRT in the near future. Panelists forecast increased software development and use of the WWW for the following: marketing of counseling services; demographic databases for research and statistics; electronic test administration, scoring, and diagnosis, as well as development of more self-assessment software; activities related to consultation and referral, supervision/training, and professional development; and therapy, both professionally and through psychoeducation/self-help. In addition, panelists indicated their beliefs that:

(1) audio/visual equipment will become more commonplace in web communications, and

(2) expressed more optimism toward security issues related to future CRT use. Although not explicitly stated by panelists, the occurrence of these two forecasts would alleviate most of the current objections to web use in therapy, and may explain the significant increase in future ratings of CRT use for therapeutic interventions/counseling/therapy work-related activities.

Experts of the study expressed their beliefs that the following conditions exist in professional counseling concerning current and future use of CRT:

CRT is currently an important and highly utilized part of professional counseling. The results of the study suggest counselors are using a wide variety of CRT tools to accomplish tasks in many different aspects of the work they perform in helping others.

The use of CRT by professional counselors will continue to increase to the extent that by 2008, almost all aspects of the work counselors do will be accomplished with the help of CRT. Counselor education programs need to recognize the importance of CRT use by professional counselors in the work they do. There has been a plea for more CRT skills training of student and professional counselors. Counselor education programs are not currently incorporating minimal computer literacy standards or providing coursework to optimally train counselors in technological skills. Counselors will need these skills in order to be proactive in developing the professional roles they play in the future.

Counselors are not currently receiving the training they need to utilize the technology available to them in ways that could result in making counselor tasks easier to perform and able to be more efficiently accomplished, and result in the production of qualitatively better service delivery. Programs that are not providing adequate CRT skills evaluation are producing graduates who begin their work as professional counselors at a distinct disadvantage to other health care providers endowed with appropriate technological skills. Those graduates must be burdened with the task of acquiring the technological skills they need on their own, in whatever haphazard manner they can, depending on available time and resources.

Although counselors are currently using CRT in limited ways to accomplish tasks involving therapeutic intervention, it is realistic to expect more extensive use of CRT in therapeutic tasks in the near future. This presents counseling professionals with the need to conduct research investigating potential effects CRT use may have on the therapeutic process. The literature is replete with calls for research to investigate potential important differences between therapeutic work accomplished with the help of CRT, as well as therapy conducted in more traditional ways in which technology is not utilized.

Increasing use of CRT offers both challenges and opportunities for us to expand the understanding of the therapeutic process by requiring us to closely examine which aspects of effective therapeutic intervention are uniquely "human" and why. This understanding can help us develop objective criteria for training mental health professionals to help others, as well as provide us with valuable information concerning which techniques clients can learn to help themselves. In addition, by more precisely defining the processes of therapeutic intervention, counselors can more objectively measure outcome effectiveness associated with a given technique.

Information literacy of counselors

Information literacy requires knowing how to access information effectively and efficiently. In this Information Age, to provide the best service to their clients and to promote their own lifelong learning, counselors need to develop information literacy. The American Library Association (ALA) has defined information literacy as having abilities to "recognize when information is needed and to locate, evaluate, and use effectively the needed information." Being able to access information effectively and efficiently is one of ALA's standards for an information literate individual.

Psychologists, whose work settings are often similar to those of counselors, have reported that to carry out their job responsibilities they often needed information, and that they had to find it themselves. The Association for Counselor Education and Supervision (ACES) Guidelines for Technical Competencies for Counselor Education Students recommend counseling students should be able

(a) to help clients search for various types of counseling-related information via the Internet...

(b) to access and use counseling related... data bases,

(c) to use the Internet for finding and using continuing education opportunities in counseling, and

(d) to evaluate the quality of Internet information.

The US Council for Accreditation of Counseling and Related Educational Programs standards indicate counselors should be familiar with the counseling research and literature by specifying that counseling programs must demonstrate application of research data and include instruction in technological competence and computer literacy. Sexton called for more emphasis on research training in counselor education, having noted earlier that counseling practitioners must be aware of what research is available. There can be no doubt that counselors need to become information literate to provide the best services to their clients and to promote their own lifelong learning. The Internet has created an increased number of sources from which counselors can access and learn about counseling research and obtain information to help their clients. However, counselors may not feel sufficiently prepared to identify and utilize them.

Graduate students reported that they feel unprepared to fully utilize library resources and insufficient attention had been given to bibliographic instruction. Various authors have addressed bibliographic instruction for psychology students, but none have addressed what counseling students need to know about bibliographic resources to be able to access information for themselves and their clients.

The Internet has expanded the nature of bibliographic resources by offering information on web sites and by increasing the accessibility and the number of databases that provide either indexing or full-text of the counseling literature. So much information in various formats is available on the Internet, that it can be a challenge to find the most relevant information quickly.

As an information environment the Internet is subject to rapid change and a lack of uniformity. Specific sites may alter their addresses, contents, or even availability, while others may fail to load needed updates. The creators of web sites, their sources, and their credibility, can be difficult to determine. Internet resources may include web sites of professional or government organizations, educational or scientific institutions, or privately maintained sites, both commercial and non-commercial.

Counselors should be aware of the types of information providers associated with the common Internet address endings—.gov., edu,.org, or.com-and the new addresses—.info,.biz,.pro,.name,.coop,.museum, and.aero recently authorized by the Internet Corporation for Assigned Names and Numbers. Although these addresses are not quality indicators, sites sponsored by governmental, educational, or scientific institutions are generally more credible than commercial or private sites. Many Internet sites sponsored by these institutions provide an abundance of information at no cost.

The rapid proliferation and mutability of Internet sites quickly dates printed directories that identify them. Most Internet researchers employ commercial Internet search engines to identify web sites of interest. Reviews and critiques of Internet search engines are available in print and on web sites. Meta search engines like ProFusion combine the functions of other search engines. Users of search engines should be aware of the criteria by which the engine selects web sites and the best strategies for searching. Some search engines provide excellent online help for users to develop search strategies. For those with subscription access, a useful database for identifying web sites is the On-line Computer Library Center's (OCLC) NetFirst, which catalogs over 100,000 Internet sites and provides up-to-date concise descriptions and links to the sites.

The delivery of electronic journals in full text, and sometimes, even multi-media, is one of the Internet's most exciting possibilities. The Association of Research Libraries' New Jour web site lists journals and newsletters as they become deliverable via the Internet. While some journals are available on the Internet for both education and psychology, Shroyer and Row found the Internet provided free full-text counterparts of only 2% of psychology journals. Many sites associated with journals were promotional or existed to encourage either membership, subscription, and purchase of products. They may offer a limited sample of full-text articles. For example, the American Counseling Association's (ACA) web site requires membership in order to access the text of the Journal of Counseling and Development.

Similarly, the American Psychological Association's (APA) web site offers information searches, but it is difficult to determine the extent of the database being searched or how to search effectively. An experienced researcher will quickly recognize that the results of APA's site search are hardly comprehensive, but a new graduate student may not. A sample of current journal articles can be downloaded in full text at the site, but subscription is necessary to access APA's PsycINFO database and full text journals.

Counselors are often delighted by the massive amount of information they can access via the Internet, but they may not access much of the full-text of peer reviewed, scholarly sources of counseling research unless they have access to some of the major commercial databases.

There are two useful databases for counselors, ERIC and Ingenta, available free on the Internet. Another major free database is PubMed that, although it provides less coverage of the counseling literature, may be useful to counselors concerned with client's medical conditions. However, with some exceptions, these databases are not full text, they are abstracting and indexing sources. There are numerous commercial producers of databases that cover counseling literature and that can be delivered via the Internet through subscription. Vendors typically sell databases delivered via the Internet by licensing agreements that limit access. Student researchers may not realize that they are able to access some journals in full text on their home computers because their university library has paid the subscription price or licensing fee for them. They are using their university's computer as the host, and the site is recognizing them as a subscriber by reading the IP number.

Students may set up a proxy server through their university's computers to access these databases through their commercial Internet providers. But graduates who no longer have the privileges of students are often confused and disappointed when they find they cannot access commercial databases via their own commercial Internet providers. Various vendors have begun marketing to individuals. This is another reason for counselors to be aware of what databases they need to best locate counseling research and literature. Databases vary in (a) years and content covered, (b) indexing policies, (c) search software employed, and (d) frequency of updates.

Information literacy must be integrated into the counselor training curriculum as "information literacy is recognized as making an important contribution to decision making, problem solving, independent learning, continuing professional development, and research. Information literate people are those who have learned how to learn and that learning should (a) be interactive and integrated, (b) be based on information resources of the real word, (c) be collaborative, and (d) utilize current media technology. Counselor educators' collaborators in infusing information literacy into the counseling curriculum include librarians, who are trained in collecting and organizing the numerous information formats, in recommending appropriate sources, and in teaching library and information research skills. Librarians may also help by teaching research classes, by advising counselors in their information research, and by creating web-based reference pages with bibliographies and Internet links to sources of counseling information.

Important points for information literate students and counselors include:

— The Internet is not entirely a free source of unlimited information. Various search engines are comparable to print directories in which those listed pay for that advertising. Many information sources on the Internet require access privileges via subscription.

— Delivery of full-text scholarly journals tends to be limited to recent publications of some, not all, journals. The majority of counseling research is published in scholarly books and journals that are still sometimes only available in traditional print format.

— Search engines and databases are powerful tools to identify relevant counseling research and literature. Databases vary in their coverage of the counseling literature and need to be selected purposefully. Effective researchers use multiple databases.

— Internet delivery of information is a rapidly changing environment. There is continual development that requires a proactive attitude toward lifelong learning to keep current with resources such as search engines and databases.

Many sources of information about counseling can be accessed on the Internet but to do so effectively and efficiently requires knowledge of search engines, web sites, and databases. The counseling curriculum typically requires students to find counseling research and literature. Students appreciate this knowledge when it is infused into the counseling curriculum.

2

Technology in Career Counselling

We are living in an information age and advanced technology continues to influence the lives in the world of work and at home. Computers, the World Wide Web, the Internet, and e-mail are discussed on a regular basis. Discussions often revolve around how computers and information networks are going to make the lives easier, or replace us as productive workers in society. Some people know how to utilize current technology and promote its use unabashedly. Other people are scared of the technology for it means change. Consequently, differing views on how this technology and information focused society will effect the world of work, and thus career counseling, have been expressed. Whereas some people may be strongly in favor of anything technological and promote technological change, others show fear regarding technology.

However, this is not the first major change in the world of work, we have survived other major changes. For example, we have moved from a society based on agriculture to industry and manufacturing to the current technological and information based society. Consequently, with planning, the society can survive and thrive while we experience technological change. We are in what is now called the Third Frontier or the Technological Revolution. Planning is needed to place technology in a context for proper use or the possible benefits of using the newfound technology will be lost, or at least minimized. This is especially so within the field of career counseling. Counselors need to become electronically and technologically competent to appreciate career development, job hunting, and employment difficulties in the twenty-first century. However, it is warned that technology cannot replace basic career counseling skills for a number of reasons. Acknowledging the impact of technology on career counseling, Internet resources are provided for use by counseling professionals and clients in conjunction with professionals.

The proper use of technology is a topic for debate especially within the counseling field. Indeed, since the introduction of technology into the counseling arena there have been supporters and detractors. For instance, one of the first to highlight some of the advantages of recording and replaying therapy sessions for supervision purposes was Carl Rogers. At the time, tape recorders were new technology and the use of audiotapes was met with some controversy. Similarly, the use of computers in therapy for client scheduling, intake interviewing, testing, and biofeedback was considered very controversial over a decade ago.

The main controversies regarding the use of technology in counseling, and specifically career counseling involves the use of computers to provide career guidance counseling and the use of the Internet in career counseling. Underlying these controversies, however, is a more fundamental issue, the purpose of career counseling. Thus, the purpose of career counseling will be discussed as the use of computers and the Internet in career counseling is explored.

The use of technology in career counseling will depend on the focus of career counseling. If we focus most on assisting individuals to make educational and vocational decisions, the greatest need may be for good data or information to make good decisions. This may include self-assessment of one's interests and values along with information regarding the current world of work. Computers can definitely help provide the information needed to make decisions. Complete and accurate as well as easily accessible data files on occupations can be found via computers.

Computers could provide the information needed to make what Parsons labeled as true reasoning. Indeed, information regarding the changing career market and resources for training may be better provided by computers due to the overwhelming amount of career information a career counselor would have to obtain to be helpful. The career counseling and guidance profession has seemingly indicated its acceptance of this use of computer technology within career counseling, as many colleges and universities and government centers now use career information delivery systems.

The use of computers to store and provide easy access to a multitude of occupational information could be said to have revolutionized the provision of career counseling. The computer guidance programs most often cited in use are the System for Assessment and Group Evaluation (SAGE), Computerized Career Assessment and Planning Program (CCAPP), Inquiry, Discover, SIGI, and SIGI Plus programs. These programs often include a large data bank of information on educational, leisure, and occupational opportunities. They often will also include a self-assessment component and are viewed as cost efficient.

It is important to have decision making skills and not just access to information. Consequently, some computer guidance programs also involve modules designed to help someone become a better decision maker and problem solver. Computers have been said to be able to help train clients to be more proficient decision makers via providing instruction with the decision making process. It is with the decision making process that controversy can enter into the use of computers within career counseling.

Interaction and feedback are important when one is making decisions and that one could use simulation games to aid in the development of decision making skills. However, one could argue that computers cannot provide appropriate interpersonal learning and that people could also easily ignore computer prompts regarding deeper thinking about a career decision. Similarly, the context in which a decision is made can have important implications for the decision-maker.

Can a computer be aware of context issues and the different complexities that context can bring to a career decision? As career counselors do not simply provide information to clients, in a 'test-and-tell' fashion, but they also guide and support and motivate people during their career transitions and decision making process.

If one conceptualizes career counseling, as also involving more personal counseling aspects, in addition to making career decisions, then the use of computers within career counseling is even more limited. For instance, career counseling may also involve discussions of balancing work and family obligations, reactions to sexual harassment, stress due to work, discrimination in the work force, bias, and pay inequities. Issues involving grief over the loss of a job and unemployment may also be addressed in career counseling. Similarly, many career counselors see career guidance as a lifelong process that involves effective general counseling skills. A computer is not currently able to adequately discuss a multitude of complex issues in a caring and interactive manner with clients in differing contexts with different personal backgrounds.

If computers are used for career decision making and advancing one's decision-making skills without the aid of a career counselor, problems can occur. Computers are often seen as faultless and accurate. Thus, those who use computers for career decision making may mistakenly believe that the computer test is telling one what to do unequivocally. This could promote decision making without attention to within-occupational variance and thus ignore personal variables effecting the career decision making process and/or career difficulty.

Few career centers require or recommend placement officer interviews for those using computer guidance systems. This is despite the fact that students have indicated preferring structured interventions when using computers versus independent computer use. Thus, the need to utilize computers as tools within career counseling in a structured and comprehensive manner is highlighted. Computers can not replace counselors but can be used as tools within career counseling.

Computers can be very helpful in career counseling in the area of providing up to date occupational data.

Assessments may also be expediently conducted via computers. However, the assessment of personal interests and abilities via computer can be tricky as the interpretation of low scores needs to be nonjudgmental and appropriate interpretation often requires clinical skill. Computers can be programmed with information but as of yet are not readily capable of highly applicable and flexible clinical skills.

The Internet and the availability of career counseling resources on the World Wide Web (WWW) and via e-mail is the second main current controversy regarding the use of technology in career counseling. The Internet is quickly becoming a revolutionary force in everyday private and business life. As reported by Mangelsdorf "call it a revolution. For better or worse, 1994 marked the year the on-line world, after quietly building momentum for years, finally hit the popular consciousness."

The Internet has the ability to quickly revolutionize the provision of career counseling. the Internet one can send and receive e-mail from individuals and subscription lists devoted to various topics were people e-mail each other as a group. In addition, one can view images and read text on individual World Wide Web (WWW) sites. The WWW is defined as a "global system of computer networks linked together by hypertext links that allow a user to jump from any place on the Web to another place on the Web." Many of the interest assessment devices and occupational data bases available via computer based systems, such as those previously discussed, are now available on-line via the Internet. Thus, the benefits and possible drawbacks of providing this information via computer apply to the provision of this information via the Internet. For instance, whereas one can have access to timely employment data on-line one could also miss the interpersonal aspects of counselor-client interaction.

The Internet can be used as a tool in career counseling to help clients investigate their interests, career options, employment statistics, and educational as well as occupational opportunities.

The need for career counselor involvement with clients as they use the Internet as a resource exists for many of the reasons career counselors advocate their involvement with clients using the previously described computer systems. The need for career counselor involvement may also be increased due to the fear some people have of computers and the lack of access some may have to computers. There is also a danger of information overload as so much information can be available on-line. One may additionally require assistance in evaluating Internet material as all Internet resources are not necessarily of high quality. Moreover, certain clients could also unwittingly become behaviorally addicted to Internet use. Internet addiction is currently a topic being researched. In addition, as feelings of isolation have been shown to increase with Internet use, the interpersonal relationship a client has with a career counselor could be doubly important.

The Internet can aid in career development and employment hunting in some additional ways.

First, as many employers are interested in hiring workers who are technologically literate, counseling clients using the Internet as a tool not only helps with the presenting career problems clients bring to session but also teaches clients a new and marketable skill: technological literacy.

Second, many people have made connections and thus network well on-line. However, one must remember that this does not diminish the importance of real life networking.

Third, many jobs are posted on-line and consequently one could have access to a larger job market if they are able to investigate Internet resources. However, once again one must be warned that not all jobs will be advertised on-line.

Fourth, clients can computerize their resume and candidate data and post this information on the Internet for employers to seek out.

Finally, clients can investigate possible employers for company stability and policies that may effect their satisfaction with a position within the agency.

Large amounts of employment information and career connections can be obtained and cultivated on the Internet if one knows where to look and has the support needed to evaluate and use this information. Internet fluency provides the career counselor with a highly interactive mode of communication and potentially up-to-date sources of information. Career counselors are in a perfect position to utilize these resources for their client's benefit. However, to do this effectively counselors must be technologically literate themselves.

Technology is listed as one of the 11 categories of minimum competence for the professional practice of career counseling. The need for students to use electronic communication technologies effectively exists. The question is not whether to use technology, but how to use it to best advantage given the setting in which one works" and the settings now include computers and the Internet.

Internet applications and careers guidance

The Internet could have massive implications for careers guidance. It has the potential to make careers information more accessible than ever before. It could also lead to new careers education and guidance practices. Technically, information can be sent via any available route across the Internet and users can follow their own pathways. In a careers context, this can increase the scope of their ideas about opportunities, encourage lateral thinking about what might be of interest, and appeal to those who see serendipity as an important part of career learning and development. At the same time, quality information providers can structure their sites to make it easy to focus on what is of value and to give access to more traditionally structured databases.

Access to Information

The Internet offers an unmediated link between user and information provider. Information can be stored as close to its source as possible, facilitating regular updating. However, the sheer quantity of unfiltered information can make it difficult for users to find and evaluate the information they need. There is a role for guidance services in providing a filter, a quality assurance process, as the number of apparently relevant sites delivered with each trawl of the Web becomes ever larger.

Direct access to computer-assisted guidance

Through file transfer or direct access to remote databases, the Internet could make it possible to access the full range of computer-assisted guidance systems `on-line', not just what happens to be available in the local school/ college or careers centre. Such systems might then be used without mediation or support from a guidance worker. The Web Site of CSU (Software Support) Ltd gives on-line access from anywhere in the world to occupational profiles from the AGCAS (Association of Graduate Careers Advisory Services) database, plus an extensive postgraduate study database. Users can also search the database of employers of graduates - SCAN on-line for information on employment relevant to their degree, desired location and choice of work etc. Information can be down-loaded or printed out.

Individual guidance at a distance

Counselling via e-mail is already being used: Chat mode allows two E-mail users to view the text sent and received simultaneously (a whole conversation on screen). For those who are shy of talking to new people about their concerns, distance contact provides a 'warm-up': a safe way to sample the relationship with the counsellor before embarking on personal contact.

Especially if coupled with (video) conferencing techniques, the Internet can provide a powerful medium for delivering distance guidance. It is even possible to see and talk with someone while viewing or using the programs on their computer. The Department for Education and Employment in UK, sponsored two programmes in 1996 involving videoconferencing to deliver guidance at a distance. One involves the adviser and client sharing the experience of doing a computer-assisted guidance program via the video-conferencing link. The adviser can discuss the results with the client and alter items in the result as needed. The other offers a video-conferencing link to the careers adviser for advice to support the use of computer-assisted guidance. Either of these activities could easily be carried on via the Internet, though video-conferencing may require a more expensive ISDN phoneline than normal internet usage.

New forms of group work

E-mail and newsgroups make possible new forms of group guidance. Anyone who registers with a newsgroup can read all letters and information posted by others, and respond or comment themselves. This offers a forum for group discussion of an issue. Extending a guidance service on to the Internet enables it to reach people in new ways and new places (including their own homes and workplaces) 24 hours a day. Conferencing facilities and the use of E-mail and newsgroups to spread information, ideas and skills, all contribute to this. At present many of the people guidance services target, when they engage in outreach, do not have access to the hardware and software needed. If this can be overcome (e.g. by providing workstations in public access points, community centres or 'telecottages') there may be particular potential for guidance via the Internet in rural, scattered communities, and for disabled or disaffected clients.

The Internet offers a speeding up and streamlining of the process of application and recruitment for jobs and courses. Current examples include:

— Electronic posting of vacancy information
— Electronic application forms

— Electronic submission of CVs and resumes

— Sites that teach job-seeking skills.

The ability to update on-line on Internet is an advantage of the clearing vacancy service offered by Hobsons on their Web site. Users can browse the data, and register an interest with an institution, giving more information about results, level of course required and so on. Alternatively, they can go from there to the institution's own home page on the World Wide Web for information. If more and more employers take to handling their recruitment via electronic media this will have considerable implications for guidance and employment services. The ability of job seekers to handle electronic applications and write effective electronic CVs and resumes will need to be supported by guidance and placement services requiring new techniques and skills. Employment services on the Internet mean the jobseeker can directly search a database of jobs for relevant vacancies, and may add his/herr own details to a central database of CVs and resumes. Employers then search the database for suitable applicants, sometimes using a computerised search of CVs to shortlist candidates. Some major employment services also offer links to other employment agencies.

Careers education programmes can offer opportunities for students to learn how to use the Internet critically and analytically to meet their own careers guidance needs. This includes teaching students to develop their own sense of quality, enabling them to make sound critical judgements about what information is offered and how to use imperfect information. These are key skills in career learning, increasing students' ability to use this medium for careers purposes will also add to their competence in other areas.

Using Intranet as well as Internet means that students can record their own experiences and learn from each other's, becoming actively involved in the creation of learning material rather than passive recipients of it. An Intranet can link schools, colleges, the careers service and students across a local network. How it works depends on the software drawn down from the Internet.

For example, an Intranet E-mail system means the staff and students can exchange information and ask questions of each other via the local network. General information, e.g. local job vacancies or work experience opportunities, could be on electronic 'bulletin boards' for all to see, or a single student could send a follow-up question to a careers adviser on something arising from an interview, or the adviser could check if the student had taken action as agreed. The use of 'Web browser" technology within such a local network makes it possible to access both the World Wide Web and in-house 'pages' carrying related curriculum resources.

The difficulty of finding material on the Internet itself can be reduced by an in-house menu or 'subject index' on the intranet that offers a speedy link to relevant local, national, or international Web sites already quality-tested by the careers co-ordinator or careers service. Another relevant programmes is the 'Cambridgeshire Careers Exchange', funded by the DfEE which uses a closed wide area network with access to the Internet or Web as required.

Marketing of Guidance Services

Many careers services are developing home pages through which they market their services to potential clients. Nearly all higher education careers services are now using the Internet for communicating with their clients. Other careers services, too, are also investing in the new communications medium. This offers public relations benefits as well as access to new groups of guidance seekers. A CSU/AGCAS survey in 1996 showed that most career-minded higher education students use the Internet regularly; a third have already used the Internet for a careers-related purpose and over 90% are interested in doing so. Students' use of the Internet is not limited to those studying for 'technical" degree subjects. Respondents' priorities were 'Up-to-date job vacancies', 'Background information on employers', General information on career choice, and 'Job applications via Internet'.

Internet and Intranet applications, 'conferencing' facilities, E-mail and newsgroups can be used to share information and good practice between professionals. Information on staff training opportunities, downloadable policy documents, quality-assurance materials, etc. can all be distributed this way. National or local labour market information can also be collated, structured, and disseminated to update advisers and support guidance. Within a local network, each individual can have a 'home page' with details of expertise and experience. These pages can be linked together to provide a training resource for others in the network. Typical users of the Net are relatively better-off, younger people, and more likely to be men than women. How can equitable access be assured to the resources of the Internet? Possible strategies include:

— *Providing more public access points*—particularly in places where people meet for other purposes. One model for this is the so-called 'Cyber-cafe', where an informal atmosphere and leisure facilities are offered alongside Internet workstations open to all.

- Linking to other guidance access points such as the national guidance helpline or local TEC/LEC training databases, or to phone in programmes on local radio or TV.
- Linking use of the Internet with use of other resources. Thus printed media or CD-ROM can be distributed which can either be used alone or enhanced by support from a World Wide Web site or via E-mail / newsgroup.

A major issue for the future is whether the Internet is to remain largely free-access or will become more commercialised. Business use is likely to increase with charges for access to some information. At present the main costs are:

- the cost of hardware—typically a modem for connecting the computer to the telephone line. If ISDN is used this will be a large additional expense;
- initial registration with, and monthly subscription to, a local service provider;
- the additional cost of renting Web space if a home page is to be set up for the school, college or guidance service, along with any programming costs involved;
- running and maintenance costs, including on-line telephone charges, usually at local rates;
- possibly some software costs, though software can often be downloaded free from the Internet or comes as part of the package from the service provider;
- staff time and training to use the system;

— the provision or hire of physical locations where the system can be used.

The number of people using the Internet is growing exponentially; because of the increased use of pictures and sound, the volume of traffic per user is growing even faster. This means a choice between expensive upgrading to ISDN lines and ever faster modems, or increasingly slow access times. Surfing' the Net is typically a slow and leisurely process because of the mass of uncoordinated, unstructured material that confronts the new user in particular.

Bookmarking of relevant and regularly used sites so that the user can return to them later. Collecting such sites, and material from them, might form the basis of a careers lesson in school. Similar signposting of useful material could be provided from a careers service homepage. Downloading of data/software from the Internet and World Wide Web. Information downloaded can be regularly 'refreshed' from the original site to ensure it is up-to-date, but used 'off-line' on one's own computer without further call charges (copyright issues may need attention).

Use of Intranet: Creating a local network linked to the wider Net, but fenced off from it, offers further possibilities for economy

Integration with other resources: E-mail and Web sites may be used sparingly, as part of a package of guidance or careers education. This ensures that the Net is used only when it is clearly the best way to deliver a learning opportunity, not because of the 'gee-whizz' factor. Training, to highlight effective and efficient ways of using the new resources.

The quality of information on the Internet is, by definition, difficult to guarantee. How important is it to do so? Those involved in education-based careers work may be less concerned about this: developing a critical approach towards imperfect information has been a traditional part of careers education. At the same time there is a natural desire to protect younger people until they have acquired such skills. But this tension is present in almost all teaching through whatever medium. For individual guidance purposes, however, information needs to be accurate, comprehensive, up-to-date, and comparable. Guidance services need to play a role in providing structure, coherence, quality assurance and 'kite-marking'. Web pages should:

— display the date of last update and the name of the provider;

— declare any vested interests or possible bias;

— offer relevant links to other sites which enhance the value of the original;

— be quick to download and easy to use;

— offer supporting resources via other media such as workbooks, video, CD-ROM, etc.

Security and Confidentiality

The security and confidentiality of personal information obviously needs additional safeguards on a system accessible from anywhere in the world. Again, the development of Intranet networks may provide some protection for guidance users. Password protected sites on the network may also help. However, the medium is clearly not best suited to the transfer of highly sensitive information.

The Internet has implications for the training needs of guidance workers. Attention to such needs will enhance the capacity of the guidance community to take a proactive part in the development of the Internet as a tool in guidance. Training needs include:

— technical awareness and understanding of the Internet and its facilities;
— ability to access the Net;
— use of E-mail;
— group facilitation skills of moderating newsgroups;
— conferencing skills;
— understanding electronic application and recruitment;
— research and information management skills;
— knowledge of sources;

There are few 'facts' in the area of career development and probably no laws. It is doubtful if many will argue with the general statement that guidance professionals try to help clients manage more efficiently the obstacles that life puts in their paths. In the case of those of us working in schools, our concern is to help young people cope with educational, vocational, and personal issues, and ultimately prepare for the adult world. For those of us working in the labour market, our focus is young adults and older people. Here our task is directed to helping the person obtain employment, or to cope with unemployment. Engaged in running self development courses or courses that help to re-skill individuals. Most guidance programmes try to encompass two fundamental tasks:

i) the task of enabling the individual to make appropriate educational or occupational choices

ii) the task of assisting the individual to manage the personal and emotional issues that attend most of the significant decisions that people make, not least the issue of career choice.

Traditionally, guidance programmes have tried, since the 1960s, to accommodate these two functions. Inevitably, theoretical differences will influence where the emphases are placed in the various programmes. Psychologists tend to place the emphasis on inner development in the belief that career choice is determined by one's self-concept. They attach much importance to personal evaluation, and they use psychometric tests to identify the aptitudes, vocational interests, and personality traits that the individual can bring to the job. Sociologists, on the other hand, attribute more weight to external factors, such as the opportunities provided by the environment. Vocational theory could be described as an inexact science in many ways and at the risk of sacrificing theoretical purity, one could say there is truth in both the psychological and sociological positions. Certainly change, mainly in the form of the microcomputer, has had the greatest impact of all. The definition of work has changed radically; traditional guidance is giving way to guidance which emphasises life-span, life space and role salience. There is no certainty that we will ever again have an abundance of the old fashioned jobs which guaranteed security for life. All of this is presently receiving intense scrutiny in Europe, no doubt inspired to a considerable extent by the high level of unemployment within the Union.

A number of characteristics have been identified by Watts and others in relation to the evolving practice of guidance. 'Guidance is now being perceived as continuous; as stretching across the life span. It is no longer seen as something limited to adolescents' For instance, guidance is now being perceived as continuous; as stretching across the life span. It is no longer seen as something limited to adolescents. An overarching trend is a concern for quality standards and evaluation. Some Member States have developed national councils to bring together the variety of interests in the delivery of guidance. They have also begun to evolve a strategy which recognises the importance of guidance within the context of educational provision, and recommends the value of access to a neutral base from which the individual can receive neutral guidance.

Facilitating educational and occupational mobility throughout the EU will increasingly become a major task of guidance counsellors as young people seek admission to educational courses or try to avail themselves of occupational opportunities in other Member States. Guidance counsellors must therefore become familiar with the European institutions that promote guidance, the support services in the various Member States, and the variety of guidance initiatives taking place, e.g. PETRA. Most of all, they must know how to access databases that contain transnational information and be able to obtain details of educational and vocational opportunities. It goes without saying that they must have a reasonable understanding of the type of guidance practised by their EU colleagues.

As the various agencies involved in guidance draw closer, training will begin to reflect their needs and perceptions. At present the guidance philosophies of education and the labour market have little in common and this gap, which is experienced by many guidance personnel throughout Europe, needs bridging. The goal of guidance is to promote the welfare of the individual client. It should never become the servant of economic or political policy Modules which have been identified by the PETRA participants as important elements in any future European guidance model include: education and training, labour market information, knowledge of social and economic conditions in the EU, intercultural competence, knowledge of Union policies and initiatives, the theory and practice of guidance and counselling, and an understanding of factors affecting educational and occupational mobility across the Union.

In practical terms this means that guidance personnel should emerge from their training with an understanding of the political, economic and social context which underpins guidance within the Union; they should be familiar with the guidance practices which operate in other States; they should be aware of good guidance practices in other countries and attempt to incorporate these in their guidance practice; they should participate in transnational networks in order to exchange experience, knowledge and information with other guidance personnel; and lastly, they should engage in the process of reviewing their own understanding of guidance and share their conclusions with other guidance practitioners.

In brief then, the shape of future guidance training programmes is likely to include modules which deal with guidance theory and practice, counselling theory and practice, national and EU education structures, national and labour market structures, the European dimension, computer assisted guidance, information management and knowledge of cultural patterns across the Union. Most important of all, it seems to me, is the need to remind ourselves that the goal of guidance is to promote the welfare of the individual client. It should never become the servant of economic or political policy. This is not to suggest that guidance and economic/political expediency may seek to override the best interests of the individual. And we should not lose sight of this in our concern to build quality control criteria into our guidance systems. Ultimately, guidance is about enabling people to reach self-fulfilment, and matters of the human heart have never been amenable to the logic of quality control.

Career planning services are differentiated from "career counseling" services. Career planning services include an active provision of information designed to help a client with a specific need, such as review of a resume; assistance in networking strategies; identification of occupations based on interests, skills, or prior work experience; support in the job-seeking process; and assessment by means of online inventories of interest, abilities, and/or work-related values. Although 'Career Counseling' may include the provision of the above services, the use of the term implies a deeper level of involvement with the client, based on the establishment of a professional counseling relationship and the potential for dealing with career development concerns well beyond those included in career planning.

Multiple means of online provision of career planning or career counseling services currently exist, the most common of which are e-mail, newsgroups, bulletin boards, chat rooms, and websites offering a wide variety of services. Telephone or audiovisual linkages supported by the Internet exist in their infancy, and will likely grow in potential as the technology improves and the costs decline.

— *Qualifications of developer or provider* : Websites and other services designed to assist clients with career planning should be developed with content input from professional career counselors. The service should clearly state the qualifications and credentials of the developers not only in the content area of professional career counseling, but also in the development of interactive online services.

— *Access and understanding of environment* —The counselor has an obligation to be aware of free public access points to the Internet within the member's community, so that a lack of financial resources does not create a significant barrier to clients accessing counseling services or information, assessment or instructional resources over the Internet. The counselor has an obligation to be as aware as possible of local conditions, cultures, and events that may impact the client.

— *Content of career counseling and planning services on the internet* : The content of a website or other service offering career information or planning services should be reviewed for the appropriateness of content offered in this medium. Some kinds of content have been extensively tested for online delivery due to the long existence of computer-based career information and guidance systems. This includes searching of databases by relevant search variables; display of occupational information; development of a resume; assessment of interests, abilities, and work-related values and linkage of these to occupational titles; instruction about occupational classification systems; relationship of school majors to occupational choices; and the completion of forms such as a financial needs assessment questionnaire or a job application. When a website offers a service which has not previously been extensively tested, this service should be carefully scrutinized to determine whether it lends itself to the Internet. The website should clearly state the kinds of client concerns that the counselor judges to be inappropriate for counseling over the Internet, or beyond the skills of the counselor.

— *Appropriateness of client for receipt of services via the internet :* The counselor has an ethical and professional responsibility to assure that the client who is requesting service can profit from it in this mode. Appropriate screening includes the following:

a) A clear statement by clients of their career planning or career counseling needs.

b) An analysis by the counselor of whether meeting those needs via Internet exchange is appropriate and of whether this particular client can benefit from counseling services provided in this mode. A judgment about the latter should be made by means of a telephone or videophone teleconference designed to specify the client's expectations, how the client has sought to meet these through other modes, and whether or not the client appears to be able to process information through an Internet medium.

— *Appropriate support to the client*—The counselor who is providing services to a client via the Internet has ethical responsibility for the following:

a) Periodic monitoring of the client's progress via telephone or videophone teleconference.

b) Identification by the counselor of a qualified career counselor in the client's geographic area should referral become necessary. If this is not possible, the web counselor using traditional referral sources to identify an appropriate practitioner, should assist the client in the selection of a counselor.

c) Appropriate discussion with the client about referral to face-to-face service should the counselor determine that little or no progress is being made toward the client's goals.

— *Clarity of contract with the client* —The counselor should define several items in writing to the client in a document that can be downloaded from the Internet or faxed to the client. This document should include at least the following items:

a) The counselor's credentials in the field.

b) The agreed-upon goals of the career counseling or career planning Internet interchange.

c) The agreed-upon cost of the services and how this will be billed.

d) Where and how clients can programmes any counselor behavior which they consider to be unethical.

e) Statement about the degree of security of the Internet and confidentiality of data transmitted on the Internet and about any special conditions related to the client's personal information.

f) A statement of the nature of client information electronically stored by the counselor, including the length of time that data will be maintained before being destroyed.

g) A statement about the need for privacy when the client is communicating with the counselor, e.g., that client communication with the counselor is not limited by having others observe or hear interactions between the counselor and client.

h) If the service includes career, educational, or employment information, the counselor is responsible for making the client aware of the typical circumstances where individuals need counseling support in order to effectively use the information.

— *Inclusion of linkages to other websites:* If a career information or counseling website includes links to other websites, the professional who creates this linkage is responsible for assuring that the services to which his or hers are linked also meet these guidelines.

— *Use of assessment*—If the career planning or career counseling service is to include online inventories or tests and their interpretation, the following conditions should apply:

a) The assessments must have been tested in computer delivery mode to assure that their psychometric properties are the same in this mode of delivery as in print form; or the client must be informed that they have not yet been tested in this same mode of delivery.

b) The counselor must abide by the same ethical guidelines as if he or she were administering and interpreting these same inventories or tests in face-to-face mode and/or in print form.

c) Every effort must be exerted to protect the confidentiality of the user's results.

d) If there is any evidence that the client does not understand the results, as evidenced by e-mail or telephone interchanges, the counselor must refer the client to a qualified career counselor in his or her geographic area.

e) The assessments must have been validated for self-help use if no counseling support is provided, or that appropriate counseling intervention is provided before and after completion of the assessment resource if the resource has not been validated for self-help use.

Professional and ethical guidelines related to the use of the internet for job posting and searching:

— The posting must represent a valid job opening for which those searching on the Internet have an opportunity to apply.

— Job postings must be removed from the Internet database within 48 hours of the time that the announced position is filled.

— Names, addresses, resumes, and other information that may be gained about individuals should not be used for any purposes other than provision of further information about job openings.

Use of a false e-mail identity when interacting with clients and/or other professionals. When acting in a professional capacity on the Internet, a counselor has a duty to identify him/herself honestly.

Accepting a client who will not identify him/herself and be willing to arrange for phone conversation as well as online interchange.

Sharking or monitoring .chat rooms and bulletin board services, and offering career planning and related services when no request has been made for services. This includes sending out mass unsolicited e-mails. Counselors may advertise their services but must do so observing proper "netiquette" and standards of professional conduct.

Since the use of the Internet is new for the delivery of career planning and counseling services, it is mandatory that the career counseling profession gain experience with this medium and evaluate its effectiveness through targeted research. The capabilities of Internet delivery of services will expand rapidly as the use of sound and video becomes more feasible. These early guidelines will need constant monitoring and revision as research data become available and additional capabilities become cost-feasible.

Web-oriented Career Guidance Services

Information and communication technologies are transforming career information and guidance services, just as they are transforming service delivery in other sectors. The evolution of the application of ICT in the field of career information and guidance can be divided into four phases.

1. The mainframe phase, from the mid-1960s to the late 1970s. A number of computer-aided guidance systems were developed which demonstrated the potential of ICT. But the costs of direct interaction with the computer meant that the only systems which proved widely practicable in cost terms were based on batch processing. The static nature of this process and the feedback delays limited the implementation of such systems.

2. The microcomputer phase, from the early 1980s to the mid-1990s. The advent of the microcomputer made interactive usage much more economical, and also made it easier to develop and market limited software packages; its attractiveness grew as more powerful versions of the personal computer were developed. The result was a substantial growth in the number of computer-aided guidance systems, and in the extent of their usage. By the 1990s it was difficult to find a guidance service in any developed country which did not make use of such systems.

3. The web phase, in the late 1990s. The advent of the Internet meant that instead of freestanding systems located in career guidance centres, websites could be developed which individuals could access instantly from a wide variety of sites, including their homes. The ease of developing such websites produced a massive increase in their number; the ease of interconnecting them meant that they no longer needed to be viewed as discrete entities. Rather than perceiving ICT solely as a service from external suppliers, guidance services began to develop their own websites.

4. The digital phase, which we are now entering. The hitherto separate 'analogue streams' of the computer, the television and the telephone are merging into an integrated 'digital river'. Individuals are now able to access the Internet not only through their personal computers but also through their televisions and mobile phones. Greatly enhanced bandwidth will shortly enhance its speed and its capacity for transmitting video and audio as well as text.

Across these four phases, three key trends can be discerned.

1. *Increased accessibility*— Whereas initially ICT-based career guidance and information services were available only at a select number of technically-equipped service locations, they are now available not only in most guidance services but also in a vast range of other locations—homes, workplaces, community locations.
2. *Increased interactivity*—In the early stages, resources were developed as separate systems, offering only limited interactivity with users. Now, they are highly interactive not only with users but also with each other and across inter-media boundaries.
3. *Much more diffused origination*—Whereas the initial computer-aided guidance systems were developed by large organisations with substantial resources at their disposal, anyone can now develop their own website.

Resources concerned with opportunity awareness include databases of learning and/or work opportunities, with a menu of search criteria which enable users to find data relevant to their needs. The databases may cover: education/training institutions or courses; occupations, employers, or job vacancies; voluntary-work opportunities; and information on how to become self-employed. Some include relevant labour-market information on supply and demand.

There are also some examples of work simulations which enable users to explore particular occupational areas in an experiential way. Resources concerned with decision learning include matching systems which enable users to relate their personal profiles to relevant learning or work opportunities. The outcome is a list of the opportunities which match the profile most closely.

Also included here are content-free decision-making resources designed to help users to explore options in a systematic way, balancing the desirability of particular options against the perceived probability of achieving them. Resources concerned with transition learning are concerned with helping users to implement their decisions. These may include support in developing action plans, preparing curricula vitae, completing application forms, and preparing for selection interviews; it may also include help in securing funding for learning opportunities or for becoming self-employed. From a policy perspective, it is important to recognise the range of these applications. Policy interventions are often confined to a limited sub-set of this range— databases, for example. Many separate packages and websites cover only one or two of these features; some, however, cover more.

In the days of computer-aided guidance systems on mainframes and microcomputers, there was a debate about the relative merits of mini systems, each addressing particular guidance functions, and of maxi systems which attempted to cover as many as possible of these functions and to facilitate 'cross-pathing' between them. Some argued that a plurality of "mini" systems encouraged diversity and choice, enabling users to select the mix of such systems which met their needs; others that maxi systems enabled users to move seamlessly between different functions, avoiding semantic discrepancies and conceptual discontinuities, and modelling the full scope and complexity of the career decision-making process.

The advent of the Internet reframed this argument, by making it possible for websites to build quasi-maxi systems on what Offer termed a 'Lego' model —piece by piece, sometimes through links to other sites. The feasibility of developing ICT-based systems which cover the whole of the guidance process poses the issue of how such resources relate to the role of the counsellor.

Traditionally, most guidance services have been built around one-to-one counselling interviews. The models used in such interviews have varied: from diagnostic approaches in which the counsellor has analysed the individual's attributes and made appropriate recommendations, to person-centred approaches in which the counsellor helps clients to explore their perceptions of themselves and of the opportunities open to them, and to reach their own decisions. In more recent years, however, there has been a move in many countries towards a more open professional model, in which the concept of the counsellor working with individual clients in a psychological vacuum is replaced or supplemented by a more diffuse approach, utilising a more varied range of interventions, with a greater emphasis on the individual as an active agent rather than a passive recipient within the guidance process. As part of this, some guidance services have moved away from a service centred on long interviews to an open-access model, with information rooms containing ICT and other resources supported by brief informal interviews, and with long interviews being available as a residual resource to those who need them.

Individuals who are initially judged to have a high level of readiness for decision-making are referred to self-help services: career resource rooms and websites designed to assist them in selecting, locating, sequencing and using needed resources with little or no staff assistance. Those judged to have a moderate level of readiness are referred to brief staff-assisted services: practitioner-guided use of resources, supplemented by group sessions. Those with a low level of readiness are referred to individual case-managed services: individual counselling and longer-term group counselling. Estimates of those requiring case-managed services tend to fall between 10% and 50%, depending on the population, with the remainder being divided between those requiring self-help and brief staff-assisted services.

A range of readiness assessment measures, using a variety of constructs, exist to help in the screening process; dimensions such as age, socio-economic status, gender and educational level represent administratively convenient but conceptually inadequate proxies for such measures. The choice of these constructs/dimensions is crucial in planning services.

A further important policy issue is whether decisions about the extent of staff assistance are to be made by policy-makers or counselling staff on a 'rationing' basis, by counselling staff in negotiation with clients, or by the clients themselves. Such screening models were initially devised to apply to clients who visit career guidance centres. In addition, however, ICT now has the capacity to take services to individuals who find it difficult to visit such centres—because they live in geographically remote areas, for example, or because they have disabilities or are home-based for other reasons, or because they are occupied during the centre's opening hours. The concept of 'distance guidance', by telephone or through the Internet, makes it possible to deliver guidance services to remote locations, with or without direct staff assistance.

In addition, some clients may prefer to access services at a distance. Increasingly, in all fields, consumers want a service to be available when they identify a need for it, with minimum delay and minimum effort: they want it here, and they want it now. They may be willing to undertake visits to dedicated physical centres where this is feasible and is perceived as offering added value, but their decision rules in this respect are becoming more and more discriminating. These decision rules may be influenced by their preferred learning style. In these various respects, ICT has the potential to significantly increase access to guidance services, freeing it from constraints of time and space. At the same time, however, there may be restrictions on access to the ICT resources themselves. There is widespread concern that the growth of the Internet is exacerbating inequalities between the information rich and the information poor: between industrialised and developing countries; between the rich and poor within each nation; and between those who are technically literate and those who are technically inept.

In the USA, for example, households with incomes of $75,000 and higher are twenty times more likely to have access to the Internet than those at the lowest income levels, and more than nine times as likely to have a computer at home. Growing access to the Internet through the television and telephone is likely to reduce these gaps; libraries and other public information points can also have an important role to play. For the present, though, the gaps remain substantial.

Most computer-aided guidance systems have been designed so that they are capable of being used on a stand-alone basis, without counsellor support. In general, however, most commentators on the use of such systems advocate the benefits of integrating them into more broadly-based guidance services. There are three models for such integration. The first is the supported model, in which the user is seen usually for a brief period before and/or after using the system. The second is the incorporated model, in which the system is used within another guidance intervention—within a classroom session, for example, or within a counselling interview, enabling counsellor and client to work with the system side-by-side. While this latter example can be very fruitful, it also means that, far from reducing the counsellor time required by the client, the system may increase it. The third model is the progressive one, in which the use of the system is preceded and/or followed by other guidance interventions—interviews, group sessions, experience-based approaches like work experience and work shadowing—in a developmental sequence. These models can also be applied to websites, but here levels of integration are potentially much stronger.

The distinguishes between independent websites which are freestanding and may be developed by a wide variety of commercial, governmental and other agencies, and integrated websites which are developed by career centres themselves. The integrated websites are of particular strategic significance for career centres because they sit at the interface between, on the one hand, their local face-to-face services and other resources within their centres, and on the other, the independent web-based services, which provide a rich range of additional resources but can also be seen as competition. Through their websites, career centres can identify the 'global' resources they wish to utilise, and then intertwine them with their own 'local' provision.

A career centre's websites can have at least five different purposes.

— As a funnel into their own existing off-line services, aiming to maximise take-up of these services.

— Act as a diversion, seeking to take the pressure away from these off-line services by diverting users to other, usually web-based resources where their needs can be met. An enhancement of such diversion, seeking to deliver on-line guidance within the site itself.

— Further enhancements: providing a forum for putting users in contact with others facing similar issues to their own, or with people who may offer help in relation to these issues; and providing a source of distance learning programmes in career management skills and related areas. Most of these purposes are not, of course, mutually exclusive, but the choice and balance between them require strategic decisions to be made, as do the choice of partners for any partnership arrangements. Not only this, but the process of making such decisions can be a valuable opportunity to review the strategic development of the centre as a whole. Many career centres clearly start by simply establishing a presence on the Internet: as puts it, 'were here, because were here, because were here'. Thereafter, it seems likely that they go through four developmental stages. The first is promotional: promoting what the service offers off-line. The second is adaptive: delivering some of these services in on-line form. The third is innovative: delivering new services on-line which are not possible, or less feasible, off-line—which is where any partnership arrangements may come into play.

> The fourth is synergistic: to intertwine on-line and off-line services in new ways. The further a career centre moves through these stages, the more it is using its website as an agent of change in relation to its service provision as a whole.

Alongside websites, there has been growing interest in the use of telephone helplines in delivering career information and guidance services. The largest telephone helpline service in this field is the Learn direct service in the UK, which was launched in February 1998 and by the end of 2000 had responded to 2.4 million calls. Other more limited helplines have been launched in other countries, including Canada and New Zealand. A comparative analysis of these helplines indicates that some have been promoted essentially as information services; others as career counselling services. Some are focused primarily on learning or on work; others on career, embracing the two. Some are aimed at young people or adults; others are all-age. Some are separate services based on call centres; others are integrated in various ways into more broadly-based services.

The decisions made about the framing of helplines in these various respects are critical. Included in this is the extent to which the service should be offered at national or at local level. With Learn direct, the original idea was that calls should be routed to helplines based as locally as possible. This is the model used, for example, by the UK National Health Service helpline NHS Direct: calls are routed to local call centres, and are only passed elsewhere when lines are busy; the notion being that, in time, it might become the 'gateway' to all local health services. In the case of Learn direct, by contrast, the helpline is offered largely at a national level. This can result in some loss of quality, in terms of access to local knowledge. Against this needs to be set the consistency of service and of helpline adviser training offered by relatively large-scale operation. Such decisions have a significant influence on the balance between 'global' and 'local' dimensions in guidance provision. This in turn is critical in determining the level of integration that is possible with face-to-face services.

A further important issue here is technological synergy. Whereas the Learn direct helpline was originally conceived as a separate service, a Learn direct website has now also been introduced, and increasing attention is being focused on integration between the two. The website includes not only courses and occupations databases, but also a diagnostic package which provides an assessment of skills, interests and values, and connects the results to occupational families. Each page of the website includes a 'call me' button which generates a telephone call from a Learn direct adviser. In principle, it should be possible in future for the adviser to bring up on their screen the caller's work to date—a draft curriculum vitae, for example—and work on it on-line with them. Conversely, more callers could be encouraged to access the website and be supported in doing so. Again, greater use of e-mail should make it possible to sustain contact over a period of time through a mixture of synchronous and asynchronous communications. The concept of flexible usage of the telephone, website and e-mail, linked with face-to-face facilities, opens up new opportunities for the delivery of career information and guidance. It means that individuals can initially access help in the form which is convenient to them and with which they feel comfortable.

Some feel comfortable visiting a careers centre; some do not. Some are more comfortable on the telephone, or on e-mail; some are not. A further dimension will be added to this by the likely move towards ready domestic access to videophones or interactive digital television. All of these could be regarded not as alternative services but as portals into a wide, flexible and well-harmonised network of services which can enrich the learning pathways available to the individual. Public policy sometimes seems to impede such harmonisation; it could, however, proactively promote it.

A key issue in relation to such models is the significance attached to the relationship between the individual and the counsellor. The model could be based on a co-ordinated range of resources, of which the counsellor is seen as one. Or it could place the relationship with the counsellor at the centre, viewing other resources as supports to this relationship. In the latter case, it needs to be recognised that the relationship can now be sustained in a variety of ways: not only face-to-face but also at a distance; and in the latter terms, both through synchronised communications like the videophone, the telephone and Internet "chat", and also through asynchronous communications like e-mail and voice-mail. The rationale for the relationship model is that career decisions have an important cognitive component, but that they are bound up very closely with people's feelings about themselves, their sense of identity, and their dreams and aspirations.

Accordingly, the individual can best be helped by working in a relationship with another individual who has the skills to enable them to address their distinctive identity. This is a strong tradition within the career guidance field, but has come under attack on two linked grounds: that by placing the relationship at the centre, it cedes too much power to the counsellor; and that because it is so labour-intensive and counsellors are costly, it is not practicable or sustainable as an extensively delivered model. This leaves the alternative view that guidance professionals should see themselves primarily not as counsellors but as managers of guidance resources: managing diverse resources in ways which enable individuals to find the means through which their personal needs can best be met. In relation to these two models, ICT tends to be viewed as leaning towards the resource-based model. But this is not necessarily the case: certainly ICT does not of itself demand a jettisoning of the relationship model.

Indeed, there is a risk that contrasting the two models too starkly may implicitly hold frozen the familiar and established practice of the face-to-face one-to-one interview. It is important to understand how technology is now transforming the ways in which human relationships are pursued and managed. Instead of assuming that crucial elements are lost when relationships are mediated by technologies, more attention needs to be paid to how technology is enabling such relationships to be developed and sustained in ways which are released from the constraints of space, time and physical presence. Constantly lurking beneath professional anxieties about the use of ICT in guidance has been the fear of reductionism: that the use of technology will lead to simplistic, 'quick-fix', information-based approaches, in which the human element is marginalised or eliminated. Increasingly, however, it can be used within an integrated approach not only to supplement but also to extend the range of this human element.

The key distinctions now are not simply between human interventions and ICT-based interventions, but between a more complex range of interventions: direct face-to-face counsellor-client interactions, on either a one-to-one or group basis; technically mediated counsellor-client interactions, on either a synchronous or asynchronous basis; and stand-alone ICT-based services in which standardised services can be repeatedly used by different users without additional human resource cost. An important issue is how these different interventions can be optimally blended in effective service delivery, attending to clients' varied needs and preferred learning styles. This has implications both for the training of counsellors, and for wider public policy.

The potential roles of public policy in relation to career information and guidance services are four-fold: legislation, remuneration, exhortation and regulation. Legislation is important in some countries in providing the essential base for such services, but is likely to apply to the services as a whole rather than to ICT in particular. The other three roles, however, can apply specifically to the use of ICT in career information and guidance services.

Many governments have seemed prepared to offer funding for initiatives involving the use of ICT in this field. Indeed, they have not infrequently seemed more willing to provide funding for such initiatives than for extensions of other forms of service delivery, and also less demanding in seeking evidence of effectiveness. In part this is because such funding is often linked to wider policy agendas: in particular, the interest of many governments in promoting e-learning and in improving the ICT capability of their citizens, as a way of seeking to ensure their nation's future economic competitiveness. It therefore has a kind of 'face validity' which sometimes seems to protect it from close critical scrutiny. Also, it is commonly justified in terms of promising future cost savings in expenditure on face-to-face career guidance services, or a somewhat different argument - extending access to such services without commensurate increases in costs.

Systematic evidence of such effects, and whether they involve any reductions in quality of outcomes, is however currently lacking. Indeed, there is some anecdotal evidence that ICT-based services may increase rather than reduce the demand for face-to-face services—and therefore lead to greater frustration if these services are not available. It may also be that the notion of evaluating the relative merits of different models of service delivery face-to-face, by computer, by telephone and so on as discrete alternatives is now outdated. In the past, these have tended to be viewed as alternative means to the same ends, which should accordingly be evaluated in comparative cost-effectiveness terms. If however as argued earlier in this chapter effective models of delivery are interweaving human and technical resources in ever denser ways, this may be an inappropriate approach. Instead, it may be that the important question now is how these models can be most effectively combined in a synergistic way, so that they add value to one another, and provide new service-delivery options for clients.

The role of government in funding ICT-based services is though open to question on more basic grounds: that the development of such services can be safely left to the market, and that public intervention is accordingly unnecessary. Certainly the Internet has fostered the growth of an open market in the field of career information and guidance: anyone anywhere can launch such services. For example, Web-based recruitment agencies are increasingly offering 'guidance' or 'careers advice' as a 'loss leader'.

The role of the market in relation to ICT in particular is closely linked to its role in relation to career information and guidance in general. The core of the case for public investment in such services is that they represent not only a private good but also a public good, in terms of their contribution both to economic efficiency and to social equity.

Traditionally, such services have often been perceived as part of social-welfare provision. In recent years, efforts have been made in a number of countries to apply market principles to social and economic activities wherever this is feasible. Under this view, public intervention in relation to public goods should be confined to areas where there is market failure.

In relation to career information and guidance, the market would seem to be potentially inadequate in three important respects. The first is impartiality. The market tends to respond to the needs of those with most resources at their disposal. In the field of career information and guidance, therefore, it tends to be drawn to the recruitment interface, and to the needs of employers at that interface. This can both constrain and distort the services that are offered, focusing them around the need to fill the vacancies on offer rather than to meet the individual's needs. This may not be sufficient to fulfil the public interest. Secondly, there may be market failure in terms of investment. This is particularly true in relation to career information, which is not 'excludable': individuals are not willing to pay for the collection and provision of information which will subsequently be available to others free of charge. This suggests that career information services should be provided by the state.

On the other hand, it is argued by some that guidance services should not be funded in this way, because they are specific to the individual and therefore are 'excludable'. It is significant, however, that in practice the only area where a significant market has developed for career guidance services is outplacement counselling, where the employer pays but has no interest in the nature of the outcome; elsewhere it seems to be difficult to commodify guidance in the way that a market with growth potential would require. In relation to ICT, the argument for the public interest in investment in career information is evident in the number of countries where governments have supported the development and maintenance of databases on educational and occupational opportunities. Such databases can either be made directly accessible to clients, or can be made available for private-sector organisations to package and distribute, whether on a fee basis or not, as a means of assuring the quality of non-government information provision.

In the USA, for example, federal and state funding have for many years supported a network of career information delivery systems, co-ordinated by the National Occupational Information Co-ordinating Committee. It is also significant, however, that all of the major 'maxi' computer-aided guidance systems were developed initially with funding from government or from private foundations. Similarly, publicly-supported Internet-based systems allow centralised planning of the resource and service design, increasing the likelihood that different functions will be effectively integrated (e.g. using the output of a transferable skills analysis as input for the creation of a curriculum vitae). Governments and foundations prefer to provide pump-priming funding for innovations which the private sector will then maintain, reinvesting a proportion of the profits into ongoing development. This is linked to the third potential source of market failure, which relates to ownership. If the aim is to integrate ICT as closely as possible into more broadly-based guidance services, and if these services are publicly-funded, then marketisation of the ICT-based services may impede the extent of the integration that is feasible.

It is also evident in, for example, current concerns in university career centres in the USA about the extent to which many of their 'mission-critical' activities are now dependent on commercial vendors. These vendors are perceived to be using their position to remove the career centres from the graduate recruitment process and establish a direct customer relationship with the student and employer —an argument that arguably would severely weaken the wider guidance role of these centres. Such arguments may provide a case for some level of continued public investment in ICT in career information and guidance services. Nonetheless, there is clearly an important role for the market too, harnessing additional resources and encouraging competition that will foster innovation. The balance is likely to vary across countries, depending on their structures and traditions and on the political philosophies of their governments.

Where the role of the market is extensive, there remain issues about whether governments should retain a residual responsibility for ensuring quality—either by exhortation, through guidelines and the like, or by regulation. These issues are particularly pressing in relation to the Internet. The quality of websites varies massively. Some are well-designed and user-friendly; some are not.

Many give no information about the sources of data and when they were last updated. A study of websites offering no-cost career assessment found that almost none included any reference to how instruments had been developed or to underpinning psychometric data on reliability and validity.

There often appears to be no security regarding the confidentiality of client data. Little account is commonly taken of clients with visual disabilities or low vocabulary levels. A variety of strategies can be adopted in response to such issues. One is to offer guidelines; another is to produce detailed quality standards. These can be linked to a self-assessed kitemarking system based on websites' affirmations that they meet these standards; or to an accredited kitemarking system based on verification by an external body. All these systems can be voluntaristic, or can be made compulsory—for example, for any services used by, or referred to by, guidance services in receipt of public funding.

Internet-Based Career Information Delivery Systems (CIDS)

An Internet-based career information delivery system (CIDS) is defined as including the following three components: assessment, search capability, and information delivery (educational and occupational data), and these components must be integrated to assist the individual in using the information from one element of the web site to complete another element of the site. Examples of integration include using assessment results to search for occupations, or looking up educational programs for an occupation being researched. This definition is congruent with the definition of CIDS adopted in the standards of the Association of Computer-Based Systems for Career Information, "A computer-based career information system delivers integrated assessment and search functions linked to career and educational information in an environment that provides user support."

An essential element in evaluating the appropriateness of potential sites for various users and populations involves an analysis of data on the effectiveness of CIDS with different populations. The process of completing research and evaluation studies is, however, a time-consuming process. Furthermore, CIDS are extremely dynamic, in that they are continuously being revised and updated as the nature of the Internet allows for immediate modifications. The rapidity of site change complicates the evaluation of Internet-based CIDS. These two problems, the time lag in publishing research and evaluation studies and the rapid evolution of CIDS on the Internet, necessitate a multidimensional approach to the evaluation process.

The use of a differential feature-cost analysis offers a potential solution to the above problems. A differential feature analysis allows the comparison of two or more CIDS in terms of the features available. In regards to previous feature-costs analyses of computer-assisted career guidance systems (CACGS), Literature relevant to CACG systems is also relevant for this analysis of Internet-based CIDS. Examining the features of an Internet-based CIDS allows practitioners to understand the most optimal ways to integrate the site into their existing service delivery.

Let us look into a study of Internet-based CIDS, conducted in US, to uderstantand it properly. The primary purposes of the study was to identify what Internet-based CIDS exist and to highlight similarities and differences among Internet-based CIDS, so that practitioners may make more informed decisions concerning the integration of sites into service delivery, Internet-based CIDS developers may more systematically present information about their site, policy makers may monitor the developing scope and direction of site features and costs, and researchers may more fully describe Internet-based CIDS in their studies.

The specific Internet-based CIDS included the study were:

1) e-Choices,

2) Career Information System - National site,

3) Embark.com - Education and Career Opportunities System (ECOS),

4) Georgia Career Information System,

5) Illinois Career Information System (Horizons),

6) Indiana Career and Postsecondary Advancement Center (ICPAC), and

7) Washington Occupational Information System (WOIS).

The US Career Information System (CIS) delivered sites for the states of Alaska, Idaho, Massachusetts, Nebraska, Nevada, Ohio, and Oregon that contain state-specific information. While these sites were reviewed, they were not listed individually due to substantial similarities to the Career Information System.

The following criteria were used in selecting Internet-based CIDS for inclusion in the study:

1) the state provider is included in the Association of Computer-Based Systems for Career Information (ACSCI) directory and the state has an Internet version of their system,

2) the site includes components that address self-assessment, the generation of alternatives through search, and the delivery of occupational and educational information, as well as integration among these components.

Features were established by beginning with the features utilized by Sampson, et al. in the cost-feature analysis of computer-assisted career guidance systems (CACGS). As the CIDS were reviewed, features were added or removed to best reflect the existing features of sites. Some features were included based on the emerging national standards for Internet delivery of CIDS, such as the NCDA Guidelines for the Use of the Internet for Provision of Career Information and Planning Services.

A four member research team was assembled to conduct the analysis. The research team met to review the purposes of the present research and then met as a group several times to discuss common criteria for features and to suggest the addition of new features or the deletion of previous features. Developers were contacted to ask if they were willing to participate in the study. All developers agreed to participate and supplied information (e.g., passwords) required to access their Internet-based CIDS. Each developer's Web site was then reviewed using the checklist by two members of the research team. Disagreements between team members over the presence or absence of specific features were resolved through group discussion and a second review of the site for the feature in question.

While every attempt has been made to be accurate, there are inherent limitations in any methodology. First, the analysis did not examine the effectiveness or desirability of the features identified for the sites. Although a site was be granted a "yes" for a particular feature, this feature was not be particularly effective or desirable for the goals of one's clientele. It is important not to confuse effectiveness with quantity of features. A second limitation involved was the use of a "checklist" approach in presenting the data. In an effort to present feature data in a succinct manner, a dichotomous yes - no "checklist" comparison of sites was used. This approach effectively simplified a massive amount of data. However, potential problems occur when this methodology oversimplifies and obscures reality. Certain features cannot be adequately explained by this "yes" - "no" analysis. This type of analysis does not capture some of the true differences.

Related to the limitation of using a "checklist" approach, the awarding of a "no" for any given site feature is not necessarily "bad" and the awarding of a "yes" for any given site feature is not necessarily "good. " In some cases a "no" may not indicate the lack of a relevant site feature. For example, if the site administers an assessment on-line that a professional views as inappropriate for her client, then a "yes" for this site feature is irrelevant. The checklist approach was a tool to be used in evaluating a system for a specific population. A third limitation of the study involved the dynamic nature of the Internet. A strength of Internet-based CIDS is the ability to constantly update and add features and content.

The growth and development of the sites appears to have been supported by four funding mechanisms:

1) separate fees charged to organizations (e.g., schools) that in turn provide access to their members (e.g., students),
2) access is bundled with fees paid for PC-based systems,
3) access is free and granted to members of a certain group (e.g., an entire state) due to underwriting by a government agency, and
4) access is universal due to underwriting by a government agency.

There is currently no evidence of an Internet CIDS that derives direct support from an individual, fee per service basis. While these Internet-based CIDS are not directly supported by individual users, it is the individual who ultimately benefits from these sites. However, not all of these individuals have the capability to initiate or sustain the career exploration and decision-making process. Varying degrees of professional support for CIDS use may be necessary depending upon user needs. None of the sites include a description of circumstances where users may need help applying the information to their specific needs. It would benefit these users if sites included contact information for local referral sources based upon user needs.

Basing the design of Web sites for career information delivery on a needs-based model, helps individuals to more quickly find information that meets their needs while understanding how to use the information they receive. Traditionally, the user has been required to learn the navigation metaphors and "rules" of a particular Web site in order to find the information which they seek. In a needs-based design, CIDS features are categorized by commonly occurring user needs. For example, college graduates often need to conduct a job search and high school students often desire to explore their occupational interests. This approach requires user reflection and provides a framework with which users can match their needs to features available on the site.

A great deal of the information about site developers and site content is contained in separate Web sites about the developer or sponsoring organization. This information is not well integrated into the Internet CIDS themselves.

Users may begin their search for career information at the Web site address for the Internet CIDS, thus missing the opportunity to find this valuable information. For example, while developers often identify themselves on their CIDS site, this identification may not be linked to the qualifications of the developer, which is posted on a different Web site.

Therefore, consumers have less information with which to make informed choices about the quality of available sites. Although a qualified developer does not ensure the existence of a valid CIDS, it is one useful piece of information individuals may use in selecting quality sites. Similarly, none of the sites provide information on validity of assessments. This information is necessary to allow practitioners to ethically discharge their responsibilities and users to determine if the assessment will meet their needs.

Likewise, while original sources were cited in much of the information content, none of the sites provided a general statement about information gathering and authoring procedures or quality control methods. Practitioners and users must have confidence that the information delivered is accurate and relevant to their needs.

Users may potentially benefit from exposure to "original source content" via links to other sites. While there is a natural desire to keep users on one's own Web site, experience with real world content may be a valuable aspect of the exploration process. For example, links to union or employer web pages offering apprenticeships would provide the learner with

1) evidence to validate information in the CIDS,
2) a chance to build a schema by comparing and contrasting options; and
3) information on which to take further action (e.g., information interview, job shadow, or application).

The downside to providing users direct access to such content is that they can easily become lost and they may not be able to judge the variable quality of information presented.

The Internet offers a wide variety of media creation and integration tools to developers, however sites currently rely on text-based strategies for information presentation. This is most likely due to delivery issues that are associated with multimedia and the Internet.

However, the user experience could be enhanced by presenting complex information in the form of simple charts delivered as graphics. One form of information delivery offering rich possibility to developers is audio. None of the sites appear to use this presentation method, even though audio is a relatively bandwidth friendly form of multimedia. It can also be a relatively easy to produce and cost effective method of integrating "real world" content.

Audio offers additional benefits to those with visual disabilities or limited reading skills. It is also important for developers to consider other accessibility issues when designing and delivering their products. For example, all developers may wish to provide alternative means of navigation or text only versions of their Web sites for individuals with visual disabilities, who may depend on text-to-speech tools for navigating the World Wide Web.

Internet-based CIDS appear to be in an early stage of development in comparison with their older, PC-based siblings. While the core information contents of Internet-based and PC-based CIDS are almost identical, tools that users can use to integrate this information in the decision-making process appear less developed. For example, none of the sites offer the capability to compare two education providers or two occupations, a common feature of standalone CIDS. This situation will probably improve over time, as developers are more able to apply their past experience with CACG systems to an Internet environment that is more responsive and fully featured. Similarly, only two CIDS currently offer an online portfolio and keep a user record through an individualized access strategy.

While group access strategies are easier to deliver and manage, they may possibly provide a less powerful experience for the user. By users having their own unique records, tools for portfolio development (e.g., resumes, assessment records, and education) and information management become possible. One possible disadvantage the individual access strategy presents is a potential learning barrier or concern about confidentiality that users may choose to avoid. Such barriers and concerns may decrease site utilization. Currently, there is no reference to ACSCI standards on any of the Internet-based CIDS. These standards represent a powerful tool for educating users and practitioners about what they should expect from providers in terms of quality and use of career information. Rather than failing to meet standards, it may be that in the rush to make sites available, time was not allocated for showing adherence to standards.

3

Technology in School Counselling

Traditionally, the guidance programes werew considered an ancillary student service isolated from the instructional program and designed primarily to encourage students to attend college. Much of the counselor's work was reactive and crisis-oriented. Today, there is an unwritten agreement among counsellors that a guidance and counseling program should refers to a comprehensive, developmental program designed to benefit all students in their journey through school and in preparation for the future.

The US National Occupational Information Coordinating Committee's (NOICC) National Career Development Guidelines, which have been adapted by forty states across the nation, list the following processes of the career guidance and counseling program:

— outreach

— instruction

— consultation

— counseling

— career information

— referral

— assessment

— work experience

— placement and follow-up

Counseling is one process of the guidance program and refers to the interaction between a professional counselor and an individual or a small group. The school counselor's counseling skills are well-defined techniques learned through professional education programs. As certified and/or licensed professionals, most school counselors hold an advanced degree in guidance and counseling or a related field.

Ethically, school counselors only counsel students concerning normal development situations and refer students with psychological disorders to professionals with appropriate clinical training. Other facets of the guidance program, such as classroom instruction or providing information, are key components of the guidance programs. Adding to the school counselors' dilemma are perceptions that they place students in classes based on their personal biases.

Professional school counselors examine their own biases and stereotypes and understand they are ethically bound to avoid restricting choices of students. They are cognizant that students must be made responsible for all their decisions—including course selection, program selection, career goals, and future plans. Obviously, students must be aware of and understand all their options if they are to make informed decisions.

Today's school counselors are required to work with all students regardless of cultural or ethnic background, sex, age, affectional orientation, special needs, class, and so forth, making it imperative that counselors understand their students' needs.

One study found student-counselees rated discussions with the counselor as more important than objective tests, interests inventories, or vocational information. Thus, it is critical that counselors understand and respond to the needs of the nation's increasingly diverse student population. According to the NOICC's National Career Development Guidelines, students need assistance in:

(1) increasing self-knowledge,

(2) educational and occupational exploration, and

(3) lifelong career planning

These elements identifying exemplary career guidance and counseling programs by expanding the first group to include "self-advocacy" and the third group to include career preparation and transition.

Many students are disadvantaged when it comes to opportunities for career development. They have inadequate sampling of work world models on which to base their emerging career identity. It is not that they don't have any, but those they have generally are inadequate.

A lack of such opportunity, however, does not result in an occupational knowledge and value vacuum. Opinions are formed, judgments are made, and many times these result in premature educational and occupational foreclosure. An opportunity unknown is not an opportunity at all.

Students need a chance to explore and test out some of their notions about the work world. Possible career options require continuous testing to help them evaluate what such options may mean to them. They need help in translating their emerging career identities into reality. Students need the opportunity to continuously and systematically explore and test out from an internal frame of reference their personal attributes in relation to the wide range of educational and career opportunities that may be available to them.

It should be clearly understood that the primary goal is not to have students choose careers to fit jobs, but rather to enlarge students' capacities and vision to make decisions about themselves and their career development in the context of the society in which they live, go to school, and work. Furthermore, the STWO Act of 1994 explicitly states the strong need for career education and career development programs for all students. For this to take place, they will need information sharing, communication, career education, labor market information, job placement, work experience programs, counseling and assessment, and public relations.

School counselors have traditionally been expected to fulfill diverse—and often conflicting—roles. They have been called to act in the capacity of confidant, disciplinarian, consultant, scheduler, politician, administrator, and psychological helper. The ambiguity regarding counselors' roles and expectations has created confusion among teachers, support staff, parents, and students.

Some schools, counselors are told to focus much of their time on record keeping, administrative responsibilities, or crisis interventions with students.

There is little time for comprehensive career exploration and planning for life after graduation. In addition, facilities and resources for planning and implementing career guidance and counseling programs are sadly lacking. The student-counselor ratios in most schools limit the services that school counselors can deliver. The following list of tasks is limited, yet, typical:

— Counselors register and schedule all new students.

— Counselors are responsible for giving ability and achievement tests.

— Counselors teach classes when teachers are absent.

— Counselors send students home who are not appropriately dressed.

— Counselors assist with duties in the principal's office.

— Counselors compute grade-point averages and are in charge of student records.

— Counselors are assigned lunchroom duty and supervise study halls.

Few studies have explored what school counselors actually do or should do at the elementary level and at the secondary level, but counselor educators and researchers are in agreement—auxiliary or administrative support functions must be eliminated from counselors' day-to-day activities if they are to be effective in fulfilling their roles.

Many believe school counselors can be a key force in preparing the nation's diverse student population for the future. With the passage of the STWO Act of 1994, school counselors are being entrusted to take the lead in assisting our nation's young people to smoothly transition from school to work. As they comply with the

STWO Act's mandates, they must also meet the challenges of accommodating the needs of an increasingly diverse student population, including girls and women as well as the college-bound and the noncollege-bound.

They are called upon to provide leadership and facilitate schools' efforts to assist the career developmental needs of all their students. To enable them to meet the expectations of the student-counselees they serve and to have an impact in educational reform, it is important they not be burdened with any non-career guidance duties.

Career Guidance Programs

Guidance and counseling is only one component of the educational effort required to better assist students with diverse needs, it is a very important one. Because of this, a major activity of the National Center for Research in Vocational Education's Office of Student Services (OSS) is to identify exemplary career guidance and counseling programs serving diverse student populations and disseminate information about them to the field. For 1995, a major activity of OSS is to conduct a national search of career guidance programs that assist all students--secondary and postsecondary--to successfully transition from school to work or to further education.

Career development is a lifelong process which incorporates general education, occupational training, and work, as well as one's social and leisure life. Career education is the process designed to assist individuals in their career development. Career guidance is one component of a career education program. According to the National Career Development Guidelines (NOICC), a career guidance program has the following characteristics:

— Is identifiable but integrated with other programs within the institution.

— Enhances the career development knowledge, skills, and abilities of all students by establishing program standards.

— Uses coordinated activities designed to support student achievement of the standards.

— Supports the delivery of the program through qualified leadership; diversified staffing; adequate facilities, materials and financial resources; and effective management.

— Is accountable, with evaluation that is based on program effectiveness in supporting student achievement of the career guidance and counseling standards.

Guidance programs consists basically of three clusters of components:

(1) the delivery of career guidance programs;

(2) the collaboration and articulation efforts; and

(3) the leadership and support given the career guidance and counseling program by the institution.

According to a Department of Labor publication, there is widespread agreement that career guidance, properly implemented, addresses three broad competency areas involved in the career development process. Ideally, career guidance programs will enhance:

- *Self-knowledge and self-awareness*: Conscious examination of personal values, interests, and goals;
- *Educational and occupational exploration*: Presentation and integration of information and experience; and
- *Decision-making and career planning*: Understanding the interrelations between the self and the world and developing skills to make realistic choices and rational decisions.

For example, Springdale High School (SHS) in America, Arkansas is a public secondary school serving diverse groups of students in grades 10-12. Its mission is to *provide challenging opportunities for EVERY student in a positive environment.* To achieve this end, Springdale High School is heavily involved in the Tech Prep movement, School-to-Work Transition, and is one of the 19 Southern Regional Educational Board (SREB) work-based learning grant sites. It has also been selected as a *High Schools That Work* site.

The *High Schools That Work* initiative is based on the belief that students in general and vocational programs of studies can master complex academic and technical concepts and skills if schools create an environment that encourages students to make the effort to succeed. The two major goals of the program are to (1) increase mathematics, science, and communication achievement of students in general and vocational studies to the national average of all students by the year 2000; and (2) combine the basic content of traditional college preparatory English, mathematics, and science courses with vocational studies in grades 9-12.

The SHS's strong comprehensive guidance program is the key to the success of these initiatives. In order to achieve their goal "to prepare all students for the choices and challenges of the 21st century," the SHS guidance program has successfully moved from the traditional "available upon demand" model to a competency-based model. Through the latter model, the desired competencies for graduating students are identified and matched with programs and activities implemented through the guidance program. Counseling personnel collaborate with the administration and faculty to plan and implement the program.

Both the vocational program and the guidance program are recognized as exemplary programs in Arkansas. Career guidance professionals and educators come often to observe this unique career guidance program in action. SHS school counselors and personnel face the challenge of responding to the needs of a diverse student population. Springdale, Arkansas is located in a rural area with a very low unemployment rate (3%). While there is an abundance of jobs, many are entry-level and/or low paying. The majority of these jobs are in the poultry industry.

A large segment of the SHS student population are from rural, economically disadvantaged families. Many are children of migrant farm workers and have limited-English proficiency. Too often, their parents do not have the information or skills to help them make informed career, occupational, or educational decisions. The components of the SHS guidance program were compared to the three clusters of components described in the framework for identifying exemplary career guidance and counseling programs. The strengths of the guidance program at Springdale High School were validated by the presence of program components that research shows successful programs possess.

The career guidance and counseling program of Springdale High School is part of a total team effort within the school to help their 1,600 students prepare for the world of work or further education. A teacher advisor system, based on a "Career Action Plan" (CAP), makes it possible to respond to the career guidance needs of this large number of students. The CAP serves as a guide to assist students and their parents to explore educational and occupational possibilities by using extensive information about the students. Teacher advisors, trained by the counselors, meet monthly with approximately 20 students. The junior high school teachers work with students during their eighth and ninth grade, while senior high school teachers advise them during their tenth through twelfth grades.

Teacher advisors meet with students for a minimum of one hour each month. The advisor also meets annually with each student and her/his parent to plan for the following year. Counselors assist advisors throughout this program by providing inservice, offering information and strategies for the meetings, and providing materials. Curriculum units on video with accompanying handouts help the advisors give consistent information to students. The videos were prepared by counselors and are tailored to the educational/employment needs of Northwest Arkansas.

Springdale students receive intensive career guidance beginning in grade eight, when they take a one-semester course called Career Orientation (CO). During the course, their learning styles, career interests, and aptitudes are assessed. Information gathered from these assessments is used during the initial CAP conferences, and reviewed and updated in succeeding CAP conferences in grades 9-12.

During the CO classes, eighth graders begin building their career portfolio which includes scores on standardized tests, learning styles, career interests, as well as previous grades. At this stage, students get a better grasp of their career aspirations by understanding and analyzing their individual strengths and weaknesses.

In the ninth grade, students participate in guidance activities that stress teamwork, use of leisure time, and conflict resolution. The Economic Education Program—the district's K-12 career education program which emphasizes K-7 career exploration—gives students the opportunity for job shadowing that increases their understanding of the relationship between work and learning. The second annual student/parent/advisor CAP conference takes place in the spring.

When students come to the high school campus in the tenth grade, they are assigned peer helpers who—under the guidance of the high school counselors—help facilitate their transition from junior to senior high school. Students are also assigned their CAP teacher/advisor who meets with them each month for career review and planning.

Teacher advisors use curriculum units designed by area counselors to provide accurate planning information. Students begin choosing a "major" and developing a program of study, which includes the selection of courses for grades 11-16. The *Choices* computerized interest inventory, with follow-up and education information, is administered to all tenth graders.

Juniors continue to meet monthly with teacher advisors and receive career planning information. They are given opportunities for work-based learning, community service, and job shadowing. The ASSET by

ACT, a college placement test used by community colleges and technical institutes, is administered to all juniors in the spring. Those who show deficiencies which require remedial courses in college are encouraged to take an acceleration course during their senior years.

Students may then retake the ASSET and use the improved score for placement. Business representatives and counselors collaborate in developing a school-to-work conference where students attend a general session and then choose "break-out" sessions led by teams of teachers and business partners. Junior students also have the option to take the Armed Services Vocational Aptitude Battery (ASVAB).

Community service is encouraged by giving elective credit options. In addition, students learn the importance of volunteerism in the community. Students use sophisticated software in the Media Center and the Career Center to explore career opportunities and colleges. Representatives from the military, postsecondary institutions, and the community are available to meet with seniors in the Career Center on a regular basis. Students are given maximum assistance in applying for work, college, financial aid, and scholarships. The College View program located in the Career Center allows students to electronically apply to many colleges and universities. An annual event that juniors and seniors look forward to attending is the College Fair at SHS where they meet admission personnel from the military and over 60 colleges.

The SHS students who are at-risk of failing (those with multiple Ds and Fs) take part in the grade improvement program (GIP). Through the GIP, students participate in workshops focusing on goal setting, study skills, assertiveness, time management, self-advocacy, and "school survival." The GIP is conducted by school counselors who meet weekly with students in groups of 6-8 to teach them study skills and provide them with the needed support for behavior change. The program is an excellent means of providing group counseling as 150 to 200 students meet weekly with counselors in small group settings. The students frequently take advantage of the Career Center housed in the SHS Guidance Department. This state-of-the art facility, which is open to students and parents any time of the day, contains the most current technology in educational and occupational exploration.

Counselors and trained student aides are on hand to help students and/or parents maximize the information available at the Career Center. At the beginning of each year, students receive orientation on the wide range of information and technology available in the Center. In addition, teachers often bring classes to the Center to conduct career research. Over the years, SHS personnel have learned that by working together they can "do a whole lot more a whole lot better."

Counselors, teachers, and the administrators are committed to assisting their students in achieving a successful life. The career guidance and counseling program works because of the solid working relationship that exists among the school staff. Counselors work closely with Northwest Arkansas Community College and Northwest Technical Institute to facilitate the movement of students to postsecondary education. Parental support is essential in making a student's program of study relevant to his or her career goals.

Parents participate in each step of their student's career planning and attend CAP conferences each spring. This program has completed its third year with extremely positive feedback from parents. It is clear that parents who would have otherwise opted to be uninvolved participate in these annual career conferences.

Administrative support for the career guidance and counseling program at SHS is visible. Increased professional development activities and improved facilities exemplify the administrative leadership that career guidance and counselors at SHS receive. The guidance program is housed in an impressive facility that includes a large reception area, a full-time registrar's office, five large counselor offices, a centrally located Career Center, a classroom that seats 40, a room for small group activities, a large conference room, and men's and women's restrooms.

The Career Center is equipped with the latest technology including twelve computers, e-mail capability, and a sophisticated phone system. The involvement of SHS in the *High Schools That Work* initiative has helped administrators of Springdale Public Schools realize the importance of an effective guidance program. To strengthen the different components of the career guidance and counseling program at SHS, professional development activities have been planned.

Counselors regularly attend various workshops to improve their skills on career counseling, group counseling, individual counseling, and assessment. Counselors have initiated model programs for student improvement including the Grade Improvement Program and Renaissance Program. As a result, student performance has improved significantly.

Other student-oriented programs initiated by this innovative team of counselors include Peer Helpers, Elementary Tutors, and opportunities for students to receive school credit for community service. Additionally, school counselors assist students in the school's Learning Center/Night School, an alternative education program designed to prevent and reclaim dropouts of all ages.

Technology and School Counselling

Technology has the potential to enhance and change forever the way school counselors support teachers, foster student development, and interact with families. Today, we are witnessing a barrage of reports on the use of educational technology in the schools and classrooms; and once again, no mention in any of these reports is made of the unique and important use of technology by the school counselors. All policymakers should expect their school counselors to have in the area of technology:

— Possess basic computer-literacy skills. School counselors must know how to use a computer, computer peripherals, and computer-application software, including word processing, spreadsheets, and presentation software. They also must be proficient in either a PC/Windows or a Macintosh platform, knowing how to access files, install software, and use on-line help menus.

— Understand and be conversant in the current and emerging state of technology in education. Guidance professionals must have a general framework of knowledge on how technology is and is not affecting students, teachers, families, and their communities. Specifically, we should expect school counselors to be familiar with state and national technology initiatives, quantitative and qualitative research on the use of technology in and out of schools, pedagogical issues and concerns raised by the use of computers, instructional-intervention methods made possible by computers, social and cultural inequities in access and use, and the current literature on issues affecting educational technology.

— Comprehend and employ all major Internet components in guidance activities. The Internet will soon become the major communication tool available to schools and families. School counselors, then, must know how to incorporate such Internet tools in their work, from the World Wide Web, e-mail, mailing lists, chat rooms, and newsgroups and bulletin boards, to file transfer protocol (FTP), gophers, Telnet, and video-conferencing. They should know how to use the Internet to access professional and academic information, exhibit proper "netiquette" while on-line, and be able to locate and communicate with other school counselors worldwide. Counselors also should possess the skills and knowledge needed to create or participate in Internet forums, Internet projects, and distance-learning activities. They must learn how to contribute to the design, construction, and maintenance of their department's Internet Web page, as well as a personal home page.

— Articulate the implications and opportunities of technology. Counselors will have to examine and discuss how technology will change various aspects of their current duties and responsibilities, as well as the ways they have traditionally worked with students, parents, and colleagues. The paradigm shift occurring in the society at large will increasingly result in counselors' becoming more of the navigator, as opposed to the pilot, in the student-counselor relationship. As the navigator, counselors will have to know when and when not to use technology with their constituents, and how to help those constituents properly interpret and apply information gained through this new medium.

— Act as an educated and objective consumer of technology. Technology is constantly changing. Newer and faster computers are being sold each year. Thousands of new software programs are being developed and marketed to schools as the "best" product to meet their students' needs. So school counselors must learn how to objectively and systematically analyze the features, functions, and benefits of new products before they are purchased with departmental funds. They need, also, to be aware of software that will lessen the time spent on administrative tasks and permit them to spend more time working with students and families.

— Grasp the ethical and legal implications of technology. Although we don't yet know with certainty their full dimensions in the field, the ethical and legal implications of technology represent an area in which school counselors should be well versed. Current ethical standards for counseling must be examined and discussed to determine their applicability within the emerging technological environment. Legal experts should be consulted to ascertain what new guidelines might be needed when working within this emerging environment.

— Construct group and "virtual" guidance activities using technology. Synchronous and asynchronous on-line activities that help students exercise judgment, develop values, and analyze and evaluate information and opinions should be implemented by school counselors. Likewise, they should design and place on their schools' guidance Web pages Web-based activities for families, with a focus on how parents and other family members can assist a child's academic, career, and social and personal development.

— Use relational databases to monitor and articulate student progress. The use of data in planning and evaluating the effectiveness of an entire school and of its guidance department is critical. Collecting and analyzing the data should be a team effort, with input from the instructional staff, administrators, and parents.

— Counselors need to be knowledgeable and proficient in software that collects the aggregated and disaggregated data needed to review, monitor, and improve performance, specifically in the areas of student achievement, attendance, enrollment, discipline, socioeconomic status, mobility rate, language, dropout rate, graduation rate, college scholarships, postsecondary options, and standardized-test participation and results. Moreover, counselors should help make the data more available and understandable for parents, perhaps by including access to personal information on the Web.

— Contribute to the development of their schools' or districts' technology plans. As schools develop and revise their written technology plans, counselors must have the technical know-how to present clearly the rationale behind various equipment and training requests. They must understand the language and the various components of a technology plan, be able to review and critique sample school-based technology plans, and know how to develop an effective technology component for their guidance departments.

— Identify national, state, and private funding for technology. An estimated $5.2 billion or more will be spent on educational technology in fiscal 1999-2000, with 45 percent of the funding coming from the federal and state governments on a competitive basis. Districts pay for about 20 percent, and private sources account for approximately 15 percent of technology spending. All told, there is an unprecedented amount of money available to school counselors, if they are taught how to identify sources and submit effective proposals.

— Infusing technology into the guidance suite, like infusing technology into the classroom, will require a concerted district, state, and national effort. Policymakers at all levels must first recognize that technology has the potential to enhance and change forever the way school counselors support teachers, foster student development, and interact with families. While their use of technology may be different, it is no less important than that of the classroom teacher.

At the district level, administrators must re-examine the role and responsibilities of their counselors. Should they spend their time, for instance, on clerical tasks or on creating virtual guidance activities and forums for students and families? Imagine having the guidance department arrange and host a "Virtual Financial Aid

Night," for example. Hundreds of parents could participate—at home—in a live chat-room discussion with the directors of financial aid from major universities. Better yet, imagine a counselor creating and moderating an Internet listserv/mailing list for parents, thereby enabling the guidance department to e-mail its weekly newsletter to parents, and giving parents the chance to easily e-mail each other about colleges they have visited with their children or suggested ways to support a child with a learning disability.

District administrators must provide school counselors with the necessary resources--in-service training, modern equipment, technical support--and, most important, the time needed to incorporate technology into their professional activities. It would be advisable, as well, to include at least one counselor on all technology planning committees. Schools and colleges must re-examine their requirements for technology courses for school counselors and such courses' specificity, recognizing that a generic or a teacher-oriented course will not help counselors address the needs of today's students and families. These targeted technology courses should center around the national standards for school counselors established this year by the American School Counselors Association. Moreover, the as college faculty members must practice what they preach, actively using technology in all courses. No school counselor should be permitted to graduate without first demonstrating his or her proficiency with and use of technology in a counseling setting.

State departments of education can help ensure that technology is being used by school counselors by requiring districts to include counseling and guidance activities in their state-approved technology plans.

Technology funds should be carefully allocated to foster and create model high-tech guidance departments throughout the state, rewarding those schools that use technology and the Internet to partner or link with other organizations. The government can assist by instituting policies requiring that states and districts appropriate a portion of federal technology funds to support guidance- and counseling-related initiatives. At the same time, a national forum should be arranged, perhaps under the auspices of the Department of Education, allowing educators, scholars, government officials, and private-sector executives to discuss methods, products, and resources needed to bring school counseling into the 21st century.

4

Designing Career Services

As career development becomes an increasingly important component of educational systems, the issues of measurement and accountability are raised. In today's workplace, employment security is becoming "employability security"—the knowledge that one has the competencies demanded in a global economy and the ability to expand and adjust those competencies as requirements change. The challenge of preparing the young people for this new workplace has generated legislative efforts to stimulate educational reform directed at creating "world class" education and a comprehensive system for helping youth make a smooth transition from high school to productive, skilled employment and further learning.

In US, the "Goals 2000: Educate America Act" establishes eight national education goals and two national councils—one to stimulate the development of voluntary academic standards and the other to identify essential occupational skills. The "School to Work Opportunities Act of 1994" is a strategy to implement the purpose of the "Goals 2000: Educate America Act," that is, helping all Americans to reach internationally competitive standards through educational reform. Career development is a major component of the "School to Work Opportunities Act (STWOA)." Career guidance and counseling, which are interventions in the career development process, are recognized as essential in helping students to choose their career (educational) pathway. Section 102 of the STWOA states that

> "The school-based component of a School-to-Work Opportunities program shall include... career awareness and career exploration and counseling (beginning at the earliest possible age, but not later than the 7th grade) in order to help students who may be interested to identify, and select or reconsider, their interests, goals, and career majors, including those options that may not be traditional for their gender, race or ethnicity."

The Act also provides grants to states to plan for and implement school-to-work opportunities systems. Renewed interest in career development has led to an equal demand for accountability. In US there afe two major endeavors are helping schools to meet the double need of accountability and assessment. First, state and professional associations, as well as national leaders, practitioners, and career development experts, collaborated to develop the National Career Development Guidelines (NOICC). The National Career Development Guidelines offer a comprehensive, competency-based approach to career development that states, educational institutions and other organizations can use in developing effective career guidance programs. The Guidelines offer the processes, content and structure for such programs. More importantly, they provide the standards or competencies for career development at four different levels--elementary, middle/junior high, high school, and postsecondary/adult. The competencies fall within three areas of career development--self-knowledge, educational and occupational exploration, and career planning. The Guidelines, already being used in over 40 states as standards or as the basis for establishing career development standards, provide nationally validated competencies that can be used in assessment. The second significant effort has been the work of the Secretary's Commission on Achieving Necessary Skills (SCANS). In the Commission report, "What Work Requires of Schools", five areas of competencies based on a three-part foundation are delineated. Of the 36 specific skills or qualities noted, over half are commonly included in a career guidance program.

Since self-assessment and reflection are important to developing personal responsibility in career decision-making, a portfolio that sets standards and also allows for reflection emerges as the instrument of choice. Until now, most efforts to document career development have been through career planners. Career planners are usually the end product of a career development process and, as such, are appropriate for secondary education or higher but not for the student at the awareness or exploratory stages. They also do not typically provide for the self-reflection essential to an individual's ownership of the process.

American School Counselor Association and the National Occupational Information Coordinating Committee designed a programme "Get A Life: Your Personal Planning Portfolio", through collaboration. It is one instrument that sets standards and allows for self-reflection. The portfolio is divided into four sections--self-knowledge, life roles, educational development, and career exploration and planning.

In US the National Career Development Guidelines for the middle and high school levels are used as competencies for both program and individual assessment. Program planners can analyze the comprehensiveness of their programs by evaluating their activities in relation to the expected student outcomes contained in the Guidelines. Individuals can determine if they have met the career development competencies through the programs offered. Within the competency file, a sign-off ascertains the strategies and the date on which each competency was addressed. In some schools, students make the decision whether, in fact, the activity or strategy presented did help them to master the competency. The personal files are a set of guiding questions that help students to reflect on their learning. The portfolio is an organizational tool that allows the owners to collect information about themselves to use in making personal, educational and career decisions. At the same time, the students are introduced to the idea that the process is lifelong, and that they must become "career negotiators", taking responsibility for their own development.

Cognitive Information Processing (CIP) approach

Within the framework of the Cognitive Information Processing (CIP) approach, readiness is defined as the capability of an individual to make appropriate career choices, taking into account the complexity of family, social, economic, and organizational factors that influence an individual's career development. Another way of viewing these two dimensions is that capability represents internal factors and complexity represents external factors that influence an individual's ability to make appropriate career choices.

Capability

Capability refers to the cognitive and affective capacity of an individual to engage in effective career problem solving and decision making. The following conditions influence individuals' capability to successfully engage in career problem solving and career decision making:

— Individuals are willing to honestly explore their knowledge of self (e.g., interests, skills, and values) so as to attain a clearer sense of identity (Self-knowledge).

— Individuals are motivated to learn about the world of work so as to enhance the development of occupational knowledge (Occupational knowledge).

— Individuals are willing to learn about and engage in career problem solving and decision making (Career decision-making skills). Important components of the ability to think through a career problem and to arrive at a career decision include:

  (a) the capacity for thinking clearly about one's career problem, its causes, and alternative courses of action to solve it (absence of problematic decision-making confusion);

  (b) confidence in selecting a best alternative course of action to solve the problem and the commitment to carry out a plan of action to implement a solution (absence of problematic commitment anxiety); and

(c) an acceptance of personal responsibility for making a career decision (absence of problematic external conflict).

— Individuals are aware of how negative thoughts and feelings potentially limit their ability to think clearly and remain motivated to solve problems and make decisions. Individuals are willing to seek assistance when they perceive that personal or external barriers are limiting their ability to choose. Individuals also possess the capacity to monitor and regulate lower-order problem solving decision-making processes (Executive processing).

Complexity

Complexity refers to contextual factors, originating in the family, society, employing organizations, or the economy, that make it more difficult to process information necessary to solve career problems and make career decisions. Family factors can contribute to or detract from readiness for career decision making. Individuals with few family responsibilities or stressors have fewer constraints to cope with, which can contribute to reduced complexity in career decision making.

Individuals with supportive family members typically have more resources for understanding and coping with problems that exist. Family factors that can contribute to complexity include deferral, e.g., compromise career development to meet needs of spouse or children or parents, role overload, e.g., roles of worker, parent, son/daughter, homemaker, student, and dysfunctional family input, e.g., over-functioning parents.

Social factors can also contribute to or detract from career decision-making readiness. While social support in the form of modeling, networking, and caring can greatly facilitate career development, other factors make individuals' career decision-making process more complicated. Discrimination on the basis of group membership, e.g., gender, race, ethnicity, age, religion, sexual orientation, disability status, obesity, poverty, and immigration status, may limit opportunity in education, training, and employment. The above groups may also be negatively impacted by stereotyping, lack of role models, bias in education, and harassment in education and employment.

Economic factors can support or inhibit readiness for career decision making. The influence of economic factors on readiness can be experienced on a general and a personal level. General economic factors include economic trends that influence the rate of change in the labor market. A greater rate of change results in greater complexity. On a personal level, poverty and the related difficulty in obtaining housing, health care, and childcare makes it more difficult to think clearly and solve career problems, and may also make it more difficult to fund education and training once an occupational choice is made.

Organizational factors can help or hinder the readiness of employed adults to make career decisions. The size of the organization influences complexity. The larger number of employment options in a large organization make the decision more complex than decisions made in small organizations with limited opportunities. Organizational culture influences complexity in relation to the amount of support provided for employee career development. In an organizational culture that supports effective mentoring, supervision, and performance appraisal, employees are more likely to have higher readiness to make career decisions. Organizations with a culture that does not support employee career development may result in employees being less well prepared to make career decisions. The stability of the organization can also influence complexity. Stable organizations with predictable opportunity structures tend to be less complex to negotiate in comparison with organizations that are rapidly expanding or are being downsized.

Generic Sequence for Career Counseling

A seven-step sequence can be used to guide clients through the problem-solving and decision-making process. Individuals referred for self-help services complete only step 1, while clients receiving brief staff-assisted and individual case-managed services complete all seven steps in the sequence. In group counseling, prescreening occurs in steps 1 and 2, while input from group members is included in steps 3 through 7.

1. *Initial interview*: An interview in which a professional or paraprofessional gains qualitative information about the context of the client's career problem.
2. *Preliminary assessment*: A screening instrument is completed by the client, to give the professional or paraprofessional quantitative information about the client's problem.
3. *Define problem and analyze causes*: Counselor and client come to a mutual preliminary understanding of the problem, defined in terms of a gap between real state and ideal state.

4. *Formulate goals*: Counselor and client together develop a set of attainable counseling goals to remove the gap.
5. *Develop individual learning plan (ILP):* The professional or paraprofessional assists the client to develop an individual learning plan (ILP) that will help in identifying a sequence of resources and activities necessary to help the client attain his or her counseling goals.
6. *Execute individual learning plan*: The client carries out the ILP with the professional or paraprofessional providing encouragement, information, clarification, reinforcement, and planning for future experiences.
7. *Summative review and generalization*: When the client has completed the ILP, the client discusses with the counselor his or her progress toward reaching the counseling goals established in Step 4. Plans for the continued use of career services are formulated. A discussion is held about applying the career problem-solving approach used in this instance to the solving of career problems in the future.

Career Service Interventions

Each individual has unique career problems and is best served by using unique combinations of career resources and services in making career decisions. A career service intervention combines assessment, information, and instructional resources with varying types and amounts of assistance to help individuals in making occupational and employment choices.

Career resources include assessment, information, and instruction. The cost-effectiveness of career service delivery depends upon the level of staff support meeting, but not exceeding, the needs of the individual. Individuals with high readiness for occupational and employment decision making have the potential to be most cost-effectively served by self-help services. Individuals with moderate readiness for occupational and employment decision making have the potential to be most cost-effectively served by brief staff-assisted services, while low readiness individuals are potentially best served by individual case-managed services.

The readiness of an individual for occupational and employment decision making can be determined by simple screening questions (brief screening), and if needed, practitioner interpretation of quickly administered, hand scorable screening instruments (comprehensive screening).

A career center in an educational, agency, or organizational setting is being used to deliver resources and services to individuals seeking assistance with career, educational, training, and employment decision making. Individuals have the option to seek career resources on a self-help basis via the Internet or other self-help resources without being physically present in a career center.

If either clients or practitioners identify a lack of progress in the successful use of self-help resources, readiness assessment may be subsequently used to better match client needs with service delivery options. Readiness assessment occurs in one step for some clients and two steps for others.

Clients and practitioners may collaboratively decide to move from one level of assistance to another level to more appropriately meet clients' needs. For example, a client initially receiving individual case-managed services may improve in career decision-making readiness to where they move to brief staff-assisted services, or a client initially receiving brief staff-assisted services may be more cost-effectively served with a self-help or an individualized intervention as his or her level of readiness changes or is more accurately assessed.

If the request for information is vague or if a career problem is apparent that involves uncertainty when a decision needs to be made, disabling emotions, confusion, or a complex array of circumstances, more comprehensive screening step occurs involving the completion and interpretation of a readiness assessment measure. The use of a readiness assessment measure provides clients and practitioners with a common frame of reference for discussing individual needs.

Staff members' judgments about individuals' readiness for career decision making should be based on test results and interaction with the individual, as opposed to a relying on a simple score on an assessment instrument. The comprehensive screening function requires a professional or paraprofessional who has demonstrated knowledge of career development, assessment, and career service delivery along with supervised experience in the use of readiness assessment measures.

Self-help services

Self-help services are more likely to be cost-effective for individuals with a high readiness for occupational and employment decision making. This level of service does not include the maintenance of individual counseling records and places no emphasis on regular systematic monitoring of individual progress. Successful use of career service interventions in a self-help mode depends on:

— Accurately assessing user needs during brief screening to ensure that there is a reasonable likelihood that the use of career resources will meet the individual's needs;

— The availability of an effective "safety net" that provides reasonable opportunities for identifying individuals who are not making successful use of career resources, e.g., brief periodic checking with users;

— The availability of staff to respond to basic questions about career resource use, e.g., clarifying interpretation of self-assessment instruments and solving problems related to the use of a specific resource;

— The availability of easy-to-understand text and multimedia support materials and signage to direct users to specific career resources, as well as supplemental services, that relate to individuals' needs; and

— The availability of text and multimedia career resources that are self-instructional and easy to use, including appropriate readability for various populations.

Self-help career services involve self-guided use of self-assessment, information, and instructional resources in a library-like or remote setting, where resources have been designed for independent use by individuals with a high readiness for occupational and employment decision making who need little or no assistance to effectively use career resources.

Guiding and monitoring the selection and use of resources by individuals is the responsibility of the practitioner in brief staff-assisted and individual case-managed service delivery. In self-help career services the guiding and monitoring function is the responsibility of the individual with support provided within the resources being used.

Effective self-help resources are designed to help users understand when and how the resource should be used. Well designed self-help resources also help individuals identify when problems are occurring in the use of the resource and understand the further resource use or additional assistance that maybe need to resolve the problem. Text and multimedia support materials and signage can be used to guide individuals in appropriately sequencing various resources among the specific options available to meet their needs.

Brief staff-assisted services

Brief staff-assisted services are more likely to be cost-effective for individuals with moderate readiness for occupational and employment decision making. This level of service typically places less emphasis on the maintenance of individual counseling records and regular systematic monitoring of individual progress. Successful use of career service interventions in a brief staff-assisted mode depends on:

— Accurately assessing user needs during comprehensive screening to ensure that there is a reasonable likelihood that the use of career service interventions will meet the individual's needs;

— The availability of an effective "safety net" that provides reasonable opportunities for identifying individuals who are not making successful use of a career service intervention, e.g., brief periodic checking with users; and

— The availability of staff to respond to basic questions about career resource use, e.g., clarifying interpretation of self-assessment instruments and solving problems related to the use of a specific resource.

— The four options for brief staff-assisted services include self-directed career decision making, career course (with large group interaction), group counseling (short term), and workshops.

Self-directed career decision making involves practitioner-guided use of self-assessment, information, and instructional resources in a library-like setting by individuals with a moderate readiness for occupational and employment decision making who need minimal assistance to effectively use career resources.

Self-directed career decision making can be used to cost-effectively deliver career service interventions. The availability of practitioners in a library-like setting allows modeling of information seeking behavior and the provision of timely encouragement and reinforcement of client exploratory behavior. Practitioner availability also provides users with opportunities for relatively immediate follow-up of resource use while the experience is still recent. Experience has also shown that career service interventions in the self-directed career decision-making mode tend to be more successful when practitioners make specific recommendations about resource use that relate to identified user needs.

Career course (with large group interaction) involves instructor-guided use of assessment, information, and instructional resources in a classroom setting with minimal opportunity for interpersonal interaction among individuals with a moderate readiness for occupational and employment decision making who need minimal assistance to effectively use career resources.

The use of specific career resources can become student assignments in a career course. Screening is accomplished by students self-selecting to register for the course or by having an advisor or instructor recommend the course. Faculty grading of student assignments (e.g., use of career resources) provides the "safety net" to identify students who may have low readiness for occupational and employment decision making and who therefore may need more individual assistance. Orientation to resource use can be provided in class or by assigned orientation videos. Follow-up of career resource use can be provided via class discussion. The use of career resources can be individualized through student learning contracts or the same career resources can be assigned for all students in a predetermined order.

Group counseling (short term) involves practitioner-guided use of assessment, information, and instructional resources in a group setting with minimal opportunity for sharing information or for developing group cohesion among individuals with a moderate readiness for occupational and employment decision making who need minimal assistance to effectively use career resources.

Screening for career service intervention use can occur at the same time screening for group membership occurs. The use of video resources for career resource orientation (such as a computer-assisted career guidance system) minimizes using valuable group processing time for didactic presentations of orientation information. Group sessions can be used as a follow-up activity to process the insights and barriers group members experience in the use of career resources. It is important that group leaders be competent to respond to member questions from the use of various career resources. The use of career resources can be linked to specific needs via an individual learning plan (ILP) for each group member. Or, if a more structured group approach is followed where all members use a common set of career resources, group sessions can be used for follow-up by processing members' experience in using specific resources.

Individual case-managed services

Individual case-managed services are more likely to be cost-effective for individuals with low readiness for occupational and employment decision making. This level of service typically places more emphasis on the maintenance of individual counseling records and regular systematic monitoring of individual progress. Successful use of career service interventions in an individual case-managed mode depends on:

— Accurately assessing user needs during comprehensive screening to ensure that there is a reasonable likelihood that the use of career service interventions will meet the individual's needs;

— The availability of staff to respond to basic questions about career resource use, e.g., clarifying interpretation of self-assessment instruments and solving problems related to the use of a specific resource; and

— The availability of practitioners who are competent to integrate career and mental health counseling in dealing with individual's low readiness for occupational and employment decision making.

The three options for individual case-managed services include individual counseling, career course with small group interaction, and group counseling (long term).

Individual counseling

Individual counseling involves practitioner-guided use of assessment, information, and instructional resources in an individual office setting with individuals who have a low readiness for occupational and employment decision making who need substantial assistance to effectively use career resources. Individual counseling offers maximum flexibility in relating counseling interventions to the needs of the individual. The timing and content of orientations and follow-up to resource use can vary considerably among clients. The nature of individuals' use of career resources provides practitioners with information about factors that may be contributing to low readiness for occupational and employment decision making. For example, individuals' comments about potential occupations resulting from the completion of an interest inventory may indicate specific negative self-talk that can be identified, challenged, and altered. The nature of the supportive relationship established between the practitioner and the client over time may be a key element in client willingness to risk the inevitable change associated with decision making.

Career course

Career course (with small group interaction) involves instructor-guided use of assessment, information, and instructional resources in a classroom setting with considerable opportunity for interpersonal interaction among individuals with a low readiness for occupational and employment decision making who need substantial assistance to effectively use career resources. The previously described counseling interventions for a career course (with large group interaction) apply here as well. The difference is that by meeting with small groups of students, instructors have the opportunity to gain more information about the nature of student decision-making difficulties and can provide more assistance to students in improving their readiness for occupational and employment choice. Dividing the class into small groups of students can improve the capability of students to learn from each other via modeling and encouragement.

Group counseling

Group counseling (long term) involves practitioner-guided use of assessment, information, and instructional resources in a group setting with considerable opportunity for sharing information and the development of group cohesion among individuals with a low readiness for occupational and employment decision making who need substantial assistance to effectively use career resources.

The previously described counseling interventions for group counseling (short term) apply here as well. The difference is that the longer duration of the group allows the development of group cohesion necessary to confront and change typically long established problematic patterns of thinking, feeling, and behaving. The longer duration of the group also provides potential support over a larger proportion of the decision-making process, e.g., supporting members in following through on an action plan to implement their goals.

Career decision-making status

The career decision-making status of individuals can be conceptualized as decided, undecided, or indecisive:

Decided Individuals

1) *Decided-Confirmation*: Individuals who are able to specify a choice, but wish to confirm or clarify the appropriateness of their choice by contrasting it with other possible choices. For example, some individuals have a tendency to be careful and systematic in their approach to making any important decision. These individuals wish to ensure that the valuing phase of the CASVE cycle has been completed to the best of their ability.

2) *Decided-Implementation*: Individuals who are able to specify a choice but who need help in implementing their choice. For example, individuals may need assistance in getting a job or selecting training options related to an occupation chosen in the valuing phase of the CASVE cycle. These individuals

either realize they need assistance before they begin the execution phase of the CASVE cycle or they have attempted execution previously and experienced difficulty.

3) *Decided-Conflict Avoidance*: Individuals who present themselves as decided as a strategy for reducing conflict and stress, when in fact they have the characteristics of the undecided or indecisive individuals described below.

Undecided Individuals

1) *Undecided-Deferred Choice*: Individuals who are unable to specify a choice, but have no need to make a choice at the present time. For example, a college freshman taking general education courses and participating in various campus activities to obtain knowledge and life experience prior to committing to a college major, can appropriately defer a choice until a later date.

2) *Undecided-Developmental*: Individuals who need to choose, are unable to commit to a choice, and who lack self, occupational, and/or decision-making knowledge. These individuals should not be considered dysfunctional, rather they have not gained the knowledge or experience necessary to make a choice. In terms of the pyramid, these individuals need clarification or addition of self, occupational, and/or decision-making knowledge. Their self-talk about career choice is less negative in comparison with indecisive individuals.

3) *Undecided-Multipotential*: Individuals who have the characteristics of someone who is undecided, with

the addition of having an overabundance of talents, interests, and opportunities. These individuals are often overwhelmed with the diversity of available options and may experience pressure from significant others, including family members, for high levels of achievement.

Indecisive Individuals

Individuals who have not made a commitment to a specific occupational choice due to gaps in the knowledge necessary for choosing, while having a maladaptive approach to problem solving in general that is accompanied by a dysfunctional level of anxiety. Indecisive individuals are similar to undecided individuals in terms of knowledge gaps, but differ in terms of executive processing. Executive processing deficiencies present in indecisive individuals may include excessive negative self-talk, attentional deficits, or confused thought processes. These executive processing deficiencies limit the acquisition of decision-making skills and occupational knowledge, as well as limit the clarity and consistency of self-knowledge. Subsequent awareness of these limitations only serves to reinforce perceived inadequacy in decision making.

Decided and undecided individuals are often best served by self-help and brief staff-assisted interventions. In general, practitioners would rarely sit with a decided or undecided individual while he or she uses career resources. Indecisive individuals are often best served by individual case-managed interventions. Practitioners may occasionally sit with an indecisive client to help him or her to monitor negative self-talk that may be limiting the individual's ability to effectively use a career resource.

Career Problem Solving and Decision Making

Screening instruments can be used, along with a brief interview, to determine client readiness for career problem solving and decision making. A low identity score and high information need and barriers scores, plus concurring interview data, would indicate more need for staff support.

Assumptions Related to Selecting Career Service Interventions

The criteria for selecting career service interventions in the Cognitive Information Processing (CIP) approach are based on the following assumptions.

1. The type and frequency of career assistance should vary to take into account the readiness of the individual for career decision making and individual differences in information-processing capabilities.
2. The choice of career service interventions should take into account their costs so as to maximize the number of individuals who may receive appropriate assistance.
3. Group-based interventions, such as group counseling, courses, and workshops, offer reasonable effectiveness at the lowest cost to clients who
   (a) possess adequate readiness to benefit from the interventions that are offered;
   (b) are not under short-term time pressures or in a state of crisis that would make it inappropriate to wait for the next scheduled group, course, or workshop; and

(c) are willing to spend the time necessary to complete the intervention.

4. Individual counseling offers the greatest effectiveness at an acceptable cost for clients who

   (a) have low readiness for career decision making, short-term time pressure, or a crisis, that cannot be effectively addressed in a group; and

   (b) have access to counselors with the training and experience necessary to deal with the career, personal, and family dynamics associated with the indecisive client.

In some cases, legislation requires that individuals meeting specific eligibility requirements receive individual case-managed services.

Career Thoughts Inventory

The Career Thoughts Inventory is a theory-based assessment and intervention resource intended to improve the quality of career decisions made by adults, college students, and high school students and the quality of career services delivered to these individuals. The CTI is a self-administered, objectively scored measure of dysfunctional thinking in career problem solving and decision making.

The CTI was developed to integrate the functions of assessment and intervention within a career service delivery context. The goal was to link the measure and the accompanying workbook in such a way that clients might make more efficient use of their time and their human service practitioner's time, while more effectively incorporating the assessment concepts into intervention strategies for change. As a result, the CTI is comprised of traditional assessment components plus a learning resource.

Cognitive Information Processing theory postulates that effective career problem solving and decision making requires the effective processing of information in the following four domains:

1) *Self-Knowledge* includes individuals' perceptions of their values, interests, skills, etc.
2) *Occupational Knowledge* includes knowledge of individual occupations and having a schema for how the world of work is organized.
3) *Decision Making Skills* are the generic information processing skills that individuals use to solve problems and make decisions, including the subcomponents of communication, analysis, synthesis, valuing, and execution.
   - *Communication*: Individuals become aware that a gap exists between an existing and a desired state of affairs as a result of one or more external cues (positive or negative events or input from one or more significant others) or internal cues (client perceptions of negative emotions, avoidance behavior, or physiological changes).
   - *Analysis*: Individuals form a mental model of the problem and perceive relationships among the components, e.g., relating self-knowledge with occupational knowledge to better understand the necessary characteristics of the occupation or other option they seek.

- *Synthesis*: Individuals expand (elaborate) and then narrow (crystallize) the alternatives that they are considering.
- *Valuing*: Individuals evaluate the costs and benefits of each of the remaining alternatives to themselves, significant others, their cultural group, and their community or society in general, ultimately leading to a first choice.
- *Execution*: Individuals formulate and commit to a plan for implementing their tentative choice, including a preparation program, reality testing, and employment seeking.

4) *Executive Processing* includes metacognitions which control the selection and sequencing of cognitive strategies used to solve a career problem through self-talk, self-awareness, and control and monitoring.

In order to simplify the process of instrument development, the above domains and subcomponents were organized into eight cognitive information processing (CIP) content dimensions that include:

1) Self-Knowledge
2) Occupational Knowledge
3) Communication
4) Analysis
5) Synthesis
6) Valuing
7) Execution
8) Executive Processing

Dysfunctional thinking in any of the above CIP eight content dimensions could impair an individual's ability to solve career problems and to make career decisions. For the purposes of this instrument, the terms thinking and information processing are used synonymously.

Cognitive therapy theoretical concepts specify that dysfunctional cognitions have a detrimental impact on behavior and emotions. Through cognitive restructuring, collaborative empiricism, attention to emotions, and the development of an effective helping relationship, clients learn to replace dysfunctional cognitions with functional cognitions, resulting in positive changes in behavior and emotions.

In developing the CTI, the following assumption was made:

— While dysfunctional thinking in career problem solving and decision making cannot be measured directly, it can be inferred from an individual's endorsement of statements (test items) reflecting a variety of dysfunctional career thoughts.

— For the purposes of this instrument, career thoughts are defined as outcomes of one's thinking about assumptions, attitudes, behaviors, beliefs, feelings, plans, and/or strategies related to career problem solving and decision making.

— Regardless of whether CTI items refer to assumptions, attitudes, behaviors, beliefs, feelings, plans, and/or strategies, all items reflect dysfunctional thinking that inhibits effective career problem solving and decision making.

The CTI is designed for the following individuals:

(a) eleventh- and twelfth grade high school students who may be choosing a postsecondary field of study, choosing an occupation, or seeking employment;

(b) college students who may be choosing a major field of study, choosing an occupation, or seeking employment; and

(c) adults who are considering an occupational or employment change, seeking employment due to unemployment or underemployment, or reentering the labor market after a substantial period of nonpaid work.

In order to facilitate quick completion, scoring, and profiling of the instrument and avoid unnecessary delays or disruptions in the service delivery process, the CTI combines the inventory, answer sheet, and profile form into one booklet. The Test Booklet can be quickly scored by clients, human service practitioners, or clerical support staff. The CTI Profile is printed on the back page of the booklet.

In service delivery, the CTI can be used by practitioners to help adults, college students, and high school students identify, challenge, and subsequently alter dysfunctional thinking that impairs their ability to effectively solve career problems and make career decisions. Specifically, the CTI can be used as an instrument for screening and needs assessment, as well as a learning resource in delivering career services. The CTI Professional Manual provides additional details on the use of the CTI and CTI Workbook, including specific strategies for individual counseling, group counseling, self-directed career decision making, workshops and curricular interventions.

The CTI can be used to identify individuals who are likely to experience problems in making career choices as a result of their dysfunctional thinking. Individuals identified as having more dysfunctional thoughts will likely require more assistance in making effective use of career services, whereas individuals identified with fewer dysfunctional thoughts will require less assistance. The CTI Workbook can be used to facilitate an individual's understanding of how much help he or she will likely need to make effective use of career services. The CTI Total score is a single global indicator of dysfunctional thinking in career problem solving and decision making.

The CTI can be used to identify the specific nature of dysfunctional thinking noted in the screening process. In problem-solving terms, the CTI is used to help define the problem space. Career interventions to reduce career choice problems can then be recommended. The CTI Workbook can be used to facilitate an individual's understanding of the nature of his or her dysfunctional thoughts. Construct scores include: Decision-Making Confusion, Commitment Anxiety, and External Conflict.

— *Decision-Making Confusion (DMC)* refers to the inability to initiate or sustain the decision making process as a result of disabling emotions and/or a lack of understanding about the decision making process itself.

— *The Commitment Anxiety (CA)* scale reflects the inability to make a commitment to a specific career choice, accompanied by generalized anxiety about the outcome of the decision making process. This anxiety perpetuates indecision.

— *The External Conflict (EC)* scale reflects the inability to balance the importance of one's own self-perceptions with the importance of input from significant others, resulting in a reluctance to assume responsibility for decision making.

As a learning resource, the CTI and the CTI Workbook can be used with various counseling interventions in assisting individuals to challenge and alter the specific dysfunctional thoughts identified as problematic in the prior needs assessment process. The primary cognitive restructuring schema used throughout the workbook encourages individuals to identify, challenge, and alter any negative career thoughts and then follow up with action. This schema is repeated at several key points in the workbook to reinforce client understanding of the cognitive restructuring process.

By reducing dysfunctional career thinking, clients are more likely to effectively process information needed for exploration, problem solving, and decision making. By becoming more aware of the negative impact of dysfunctional thinking and by learning the process of cognitive restructuring, clients can become "freed up" to think in more creative, reality-based ways about their career choices. A theory-based decision-making checklist, included in the CTI Workbook, can indicate potentially useful areas for specific instruction in career decision making. The CTI and the CTI Workbook are designed to help clients make current career decisions as well as learn how to be better problem solvers in the future. The Workbook includes the following five sections:

— *Section 1.* Identifying Your Total Amount of Negative Career Thoughts: The CTI Total Score. The first section is designed to help clients understand that as dysfunctional career thinking increases, the level of practitioner assistance likely needed to benefit from career services increases as well. The intended outcome of using this section is that clients will be more motivated to seek a level of service appropriate for their needs.

— *Section 2.* Identifying the Nature of Your Negative Career Thoughts. The second section is designed to help clients gain insight into the development and maintenance of their dysfunctional thinking. The intended outcome of using this section is that clients will be more self-aware, more capable of monitoring and controlling cognitions, and more motivated to cognitively restructure negative career thoughts and take action to make career decisions.

— *Section 3.* Challenging and Altering Your Negative Career Thoughts and Taking Action. The third section is designed to improve self-awareness of the detrimental impact of dysfunctional thinking on career problem solving and decision making, to improve client capacity to monitor and control negative self-talk, to facilitate the cognitive restructuring of negative career thoughts through completion of an exercise, and to facilitate the development of an Individual Action Plan (IAP) for using career resources and services. The intended outcome of using this section is that clients will reduce their dysfunctional career thinking and more effectively use career resources and services, ultimately leading to a more consisfent reduction of dysfunctional thoughts and more appropriate career decisions.

— *Section 4.* Improving Your Ability to Make Good Decisions. The fourth section is designed to enhance the present and future decision-making skills of clients through decision-making instruction. The intended outcome of using this section is that clients will be better able to assess and apply their skills in career problem solving and decision making.

— *Section 5.* Making Good Use of Support from Other People. The fifth section is designed to help clients better understand how support resources can be used to their benefit in cognitive restructuring, career exploration, and decision making. The intended outcome of using this section is that clients will be more proactive, knowledgeable consumers in making effective use of available practitioners and significant others.

Diversity Issues

The influence of group membership relating to age, disability, ethnicity, gender, race, sexual orientation, and socio-economic status on career thoughts can be an important environmental factor in career choice. Group membership may enhance career choice via networking and mentoring or it may constrain career choice via stereotyping and prejudice. The specific nature and consequences of these environmental factors on career choice will likely vary with group membership. As a result, the specific career thoughts of an individual are a product of individual experience, mediated by personal characteristics and by group membership in a cultural context.

It is difficult to develop an instrument that reflects differences in life experience between group cultures, and within subcultures of specific groups, that is brief enough to be hand scored for use as a screening tool in service delivery. The CTI was designed to measure career thoughts that tend to be common across groups. In developing the CTI, potential items that were significantly associated with gender or ethnicity were eliminated from the item pool. It is possible, however, to collaboratively use the CTI with the client to identify, challenge, and alter career thoughts of an individual from a specific group. The Professional Manual includes specific suggestions for dealing with diversity issues in interpreting the CTI and using the CTI Workbook.

A variety of practitioners may make effective use of the CTI. In addition to general training in human behavior, helping skills, and assessment, practitioners need training in career development, career service delivery, and cognitive-behavior therapy. In addition to general experience in the delivery of human services, practitioners need experience in the delivery of career services with appropriate supervision. In particular, practitioners using the CTI with clients should be familiar with the professional manual, personally complete all components of the CTI, and make use of appropriate supervision.

A rational-empirical approach was used in developing the CTI. After reviewing the theoretical foundations of the CTI and the literature on dysfunctional thinking in career choice, criteria were developed for each of the eight CIP content dimensions. An initial pool of 248 items was then created based on actual client statements from the career counseling experience of the authors. After review by experienced career counselors for item clarity and realism, the pool was revised to 195 items and then reviewed by a six-member bias panel to identify and correct any bias related to ethnicity, gender, disability, and age. The 195 item pool plus 13 randomly inserted items from the short form of the Marlowe-Crowne Social Desirability Scale was administered to 320 volunteer undergraduate students. Eighty items were retained on the basis of their general psychometric quality, freedom from gender, ethnic, or social desirability bias, item-scale reliability, and content domain coverage.

A principal components analysis with Varimax rotation from an administration of these 80 items with a new sample of 196 volunteer undergraduate students revealed three interpretable constructs that were associated with dysfunctional career thinking: decision-making confusion, commitment anxiety, and external conflict. Items could then be identified as relating to one of these three constructs as well as contributing to one of the eight CIP content dimensions. The 80 items were also administered to clients seeking services, allowing an analysis of the capacity of individual items to distinguish clients (n=68) from non-clients (n=196).

A shortened 48-item version of the CTI was then derived on the basis of factor loadings, contribution to scale separation, capacity to discriminate clients from non-clients, and content domain coverage. The 48 items were then administered to a new sample of 145 volunteer undergraduate students. A second principal components analysis with Varimax rotation revealed the same three interpretable constructs as above.

In order to assist clients in challenging and altering their thoughts, reframing stimulus statements were written for each CTI item to show clients how negative thoughts interfere with their ability to make career decisions, and to provide information on making the best use of time spent on career decision making. Reframing stimulus statements include varying combinations of the following themes:

(a) the difficulty often encountered by individuals making career choices;

(b) the often inherent ambiguities in making career choices;

(c) the importance of assuming personal responsibility for decision making while also considering input from significant others;

(d) the importance of linking career choices with other life choices;

(e) the identification of factors that make it more difficult to think clearly about career options;

(f) the identification of absolute dichotomous thinking that interferes with career choice;

(g) the assumption that improved decision-making and information-seeking skills can be learned;

(h) the value of broad career exploration prior to final choice;

(i) the value of using a variety of sources of information in career exploration; and

(j) the value of obtaining assistance from a helping professional when individuals experience difficulty in career choice.

The reframing stimulus statements were then examined for potential bias regarding ethnicity, gender, disability, and age. The exercise was pilot tested and subsequently revised for clarity. Interpretive and decision-making instruction sections were then added to the workbook.

Standardisation

CTI normative data were collected for adults (n=571), college students (n=595), and eleventh- and twelfth grade high school students (n=396). Combined data on college student and adult clients (n=376) were also collected. In general, all groups were representative in terms of geographic distribution, gender, and ethnicity, with the exception that female adults were overrepresented, Hispanic American adults were underrepresented, and female clients were overrepresented.

Organizations and individuals are strongly encouraged to develop local CTI norms to allow more specific population comparisons. Analysis of normative data revealed that gender and ethnicity accounted for.2% and.1% of the variance, respectively, in CTI Total scores for all groups combined. Therefore, it was concluded that there is little relationship between gender or ethnicity with respect to CTI Total scores, and that there was no need to provide separate norms for either of these factors.

Reliability

Internal consistency. The internal consistency of the CTI Total score and construct scales was determined by calculating coefficient alphas for each of the respective norm groups. The internal consistency (alpha) coefficients for the CTI Total score ranged from.97 to.93. Alpha coefficients for the construct scales ranged from.94 to.74.

Stability. Stability concerns the extent to which individuals achieve the same CTI scores on two different occasions. The stability of the CTI Total score and construct scales was determined by having 73 volunteer college students and 48 volunteer eleventh- and twelfth grade high school students complete the CTI twice over a four week interval. Four-week test-retest stability coefficients for the CTI Total score was high (r =.86) for the college student sample, indicating little change in responses to the entire 48 items over the 4-week period. The stability coefficients for the construct scales ranged from.82 to.74, following a similar pattern as the data for internal consistency, with lower correlations for scales with fewer items. This pattern was also observed for the high school student sample, with the CTI Total at r =.69 and the construct scales ranging from.72 to.52, showing that adequate stability exists for the use of the instrument.

Validity

Content validity. Content validity concerns the congruence of CTI items, CIP content dimensions, and construct scales with the theoretical basis of the instrument. This congruence was built into the development strategy for the CTI items and scales. Individual items and construct scales are directly linked to CIP theory through content dimensions. CIP content dimensions (self-knowledge, occupational knowledge, communication, analysis, synthesis, valuing, execution, and executive processing) provided specific criteria for developing items. The CTI Professional Manual groups all 48 CTI items by content dimension and includes the corresponding criterion number or numbers for each.

Construct validity. Construct validity is concerned with the extent to which clusters of empirically associated items that are conceptually consistent with the theory can be identified and reproduced across populations. Evidence of construct validity was established through a series of factor analyses. The constructs of decision-making confusion, commitment anxiety, and external conflict, that were identified in two different samples during CTI development, were replicated for adults, college students, and eleventh- and twelfth-grade high school students based on normative data. The CTI Total score is highly correlated (r =.89 to.94) with DMC for all groups. These correlations, along with the large percentage of the variance accounted for by DMC (factor 1), suggests that a general predisposition toward dysfunctional thinking strongly influences subsequent specific aspects of dysfunctional career thinking, such as commitment anxiety. External conflict (EC) appears somewhat less related to general dysfunctional thinking, as represented by the lower correlation of EC with the CTI Total score and DMC. Correlations among construct scales, especially CA and EC, are distinctly lower for the client population than for non-client adults, college students, and high school students. CA and EC appear to be more distinct from DMC for clients than nonclients.

Given the magnitude of correlations among CTI factors observed above for adults, college students, and high school students, a Principal Components Analysis with oblique rotation was used to extract the factor structure of the instrument. A three-factor model was confirmed for the college population, the combined normative sample, and the client comparison group. A two-factor solution (decision-making confusion and external conflict) was the most interpretable solution for the adult sample, whereas a different two-factor solution (decision-making confusion and commitment anxiety) was most interpretable for high school students. The interpretation of these findings is that for adult non-client populations who are almost all employed or not seeking employment, commitment anxiety is not an operative construct when a career problem does not exist, whereas confusion about decision making and external conflict with significant others (such as spouses) are operative. For high school non-client populations, external conflict with significant others (such as parents and caretakers) concerning career problems is not yet an issue, whereas confusion about decision making and anxiety about post-high school commitments yet to be made are operative. The three-factor solution, including decision-making confusion, commitment anxiety, and external conflict, was again reproduced for the client population, for which the CTI was designed.

What these analyses reveal about the construct validity of the CTI is that there is a single powerful confusion entity that is pervasive in career problem solving and decision making. Beyond this, there are more specific issues related to one's anxiety about committing to a career choice and to potential conflict with significant others. Therefore, all three constructs may be viewed as indicators of the presence of dysfunctional thinking that constrains the cognitive system that undergirds career problem solving and decision making.

Convergent validity. Convergent validity is concerned with the extent to which the CTI Total score and construct scale scores correlate with other measures of similar constructs in a theoretically consistent direction.

Evidence of convergent validity was established by administering the above measures to 50 adults, 152 college students, and 151 eleventh- and twelfth-grade high school students. All samples were representative in terms of geographic distribution, gender, and ethnicity, with the exception that females slightly outnumbered males (56% to 44%) across all three groups and Hispanic American adults were underrepresented.

Across all three groups (adults, college students, and high school students), CTI scales were consistently inversely correlated with positive constructs such as vocational identity, certainty, and knowledge about occupations and training, and directly correlated with indecision. The CTI Total score was consistently directly correlated with neuroticism and vulnerability. Only career choice importance exhibited inconsistency in relationships across groups as was expected. Although CTI construct scales covaried directly with angry hostility, self-consciousness, and impulsiveness, the relatively low magnitude of the correlations have limited practical importance.

CTI scales for adults were consistently inversely correlated with comfort with choice, decidedness, and lack of information needs and positively correlated with anxiety. CTI scales for college students were consistently inversely correlated with comfort with choice and decisiveness, and correlated positively with depression for the CTI Total score. CTI scales for high school students were consistently inversely correlated with self-clarity.

Relationships between the CTI Total score and convergent variables were very similar to the relationships observed between DMC and the convergent variables. This is to be expected given the high correlation between the CTI Total score and the DMC scale. The number of correlations having practical significance (.50 to.75) were 32 for adults, 21 for college students, and 17 for high school students. This is also to be expected given the slightly lower alpha reliabilities for high school students and college students in comparison with adults. These lower reliability coefficients, combined with the lower alpha reliabilities from some CDP scales and small numbers of items in NEO facet scales, could explain the lower number of correlations between convergent variables and either CA or EC.

Criterion validity. Criterion validity is concerned with the extent to which the CTI accurately discriminates between persons seeking career services (clients) and persons not seeking career services (nonclients). Evidence of predictive validity was established by administering the CTI to 199 clients and 149 nonclients at two different universities. Both samples were representative in terms of geographic distribution and ethnicity, with the exception that females slightly outnumbered males and a greater proportion of clients were sophomores while a greater proportion of nonclients were seniors. Analysis of the data revealed significant differences in CTI Total and construct scales for each group, with clients having higher scores as predicted. Post-hoc CTI item-level comparisons revealed significant differences between clients and nonclients on 26 items, with clients scoring higher than nonclients on all 48 items.

Utility

The utility of a test concerns how well the test achieves its intended purpose within the constraints of "typical" practice. Many career service delivery organizations serve numerous clients. In this type of environment, an instrument used for screening, needs assessment, and learning is most cost-effective when it can be:

1) quickly administered,
2) rapidly scored,
3) easily interpreted,
4) easily integrated into counseling homework, and
5) inexpensively used.

The CTI was designed to meet the above criteria. Quick administration - most clients complete the 48 CTI items in 7 to 15 minutes. Rapid scoring - the CTI can be hand scored in 5 to 8 minutes. As a result, the CTI can be used as part of a brief intake procedure or during an initial session. Easy interpretation - the CTI includes a limited number of scales (the CTI Total score and three construct scales), which simplifies interpretation. The CTI Workbook presents interpretive information for all four scales with text, metaphors, and illustrations that practitioners can use to facilitate interpretation of CTI results. Easy integration - the CTI workbook has several components that can be assigned as homework, such as cognitive restructuring of negative thoughts, developing an individual action plan for using career resources and services, and learning about the decision-making process.

Career Guidance: Chaning Needs

The economic as well as technological revolutions has transfomrd the traditionsal needs of the labour markets. The initial effect of the reforms was largely to destroy economically inefficient jobs, without generating the means to replace them. It has now become evident that in many places there is a need for active labour-market policies, linked to economic development. Governments have to intervene in order to make the markets work. But this requires different kinds of intervention than those of the old command-economy model: interventions designed to support markets rather than replace them. In particular, it requires measures to be taken to build new markets, to regulate existing markets, and—where necessary—to compensate for market failure. Career guidance is a classic intervention of this kind. It is a means of helping individuals to maximise their choices within their environment. It cannot of itself act as a significant instrument of economic regeneration but, linked to a range of structural measures, it can provide a means of lubricating these measures and reconciling them with the individual empowerment which ultimately is the engine that will determine their effectiveness.

The subtlety of its modus operandi means that its importance can easily be overlooked by impatient policy-makers and belies its potential significance. Until fairly recently most political leaders saw school guidance and vocational guidance as a way of improving the match-up between the aspirations of the young people and adults and the jobs offered by the market. However, many people are now fully aware that what lies ahead of them is not a once-and-for-all transition from training to working life. People cannot hope to go through the whole of their working lives on the basis of what they learned during initial training.

Alongside the massive transformations in the countries of central and eastern Europe, all advanced industrial societies are currently experiencing the transition to a post-industrial era, in which the structures of work and of careers are being reshaped thoroughly. The pace of change stems from two linked forces: the impact of new technology and the globalisation of the economy. Today, all work organisations have to be prepared to change much more regularly and rapidly than ever before. As a result, they are less prepared to make long-term commitments to individuals. The psychological contract between the individual and the employer is being restructured: the old long-term relational contract, based on security and reciprocal loyalty, is in many cases being replaced by a short-term 27 transactional contract based on a narrower and more purely economic exchange; where the relational contract survives, it commonly involves exchanging job security for task flexibility. Individuals now have to take more responsibility for their own career development, including learning new skills and knowledge. Increasingly, security lies not in employment, but in employability, accumulating skills and reputation that can be invested in new opportunities as they arise.

The idea of life-long learning, which has come to the fore, has deep-seated implications for guidance. It implies a series of phases during which people seek to update their knowledge and skills—an almost permanent interchange between training and employment. These changes represent what has been called a 'careerquake'. The old concept of career was based on orderly progression up a hierarchy within an organisation or profession.

The foundations of this concept are being shaken and in many cases destroyed. In its place, a new concept of career is being built, redefined as the individual's lifelong progression in learning and in work. This new concept is in principle accessible to all, not just to the few. But it requires policy supports. One of these supports is life-long access to career guidance. This re-frames our approach to career guidance. Instead of thinking of how to help individuals choose traditional careers, it focuses attention on how to help them construct their own careers through a series of decisions made throughout their lives. It shifts the focus of career counsellors to helping people to be authors of their career narratives: to tell the story so far; to shape the themes and the story-line; and to start drafting the next chapter. This implies helping individuals to develop the skills and attitudes which will enable them to construct their careers. Such learning needs to be adapted to the new concept of career.

Perhaps, instead of emphasising decision-making, emphasise the wisdom of open-mindedness. Perhaps unplanned events should be seen not just as an inevitable but also as a desirable aspect of everyone's career. Arguably, guidance services now need to encourage a clear but flexible sense of direction, which people are ready to adapt when unexpected events occur, but which will help them to spot these events and take advantage of them.

The relevance of all this to the countries of central and eastern Europe is evident. There are signs of regeneration of career guidance services in central and eastern Europe. The aid programmes provided by the World Bank and other international organisations have played an important role in supporting these developments. Underlying them has been a major shift in the philosophy of career guidance. In line with developments in Western Europe and North America, the paternalistic care-taking that once prevailed is being replaced by a form of counselling that offers help so that people will be able to plan and guide their own lives more independently and with more competence. But the harshness of the socio-economic reality have hampered the move towards modern counselling.

Many of the initiatives to date have, understandably, been linked to the need to respond to high unemployment levels. This has dangers attached to it, particularly if the guidance is largely placement-oriented and based on a narrow matching model. In this situation, the scarcity of vacancies can easily cast guidance into disrepute. While, also in central and eastern Europe, the theory may have penetrated into the core of the profession, its translation into practice has only just begun.

The deepest roots of career guidance and counselling in central Europe are closely entwined with those of western Europe. In Hungary, for example, the first professional publications on the subject appeared towards the end of the 19th century. A government initiative launched in the early 1920s resulted in the establishment of the first Careers Guidance and Counselling Institute in Budapest in 1927. Contemporary initiatives in north-eastern and south-eastern Europe were less advanced.

In central and eastern Europe further development of career guidance and counselling services came to a grinding halt and remained in hibernation for almost half a century. Full employment under the command economy invalidated the need for guidance to be more than a referral service. In Hungary though, the development of guidance and counselling institutions was already started again in the early seventies and flourished during the eighties. Other countries had to wait until the early nineties for this to happen. In Romania for instance, a nation-wide initiative to revive counselling services was not started until 1995. In general, the period of transition to a market economy, and the resulting turmoil in the labour market pushed the issue of career guidance into focus again. In Hungary, since 1991 career guidance and counselling services are gradually being moved to the labour centres, the new basic institutions of the organisation of the labour market. Other countries chose other institutions. During the 1990s, the institutions of vocational training and of the labour markets throughout the region underwent fundamental changes but, despite extensive legal regulation being applied everywhere, the development of institutionalised career guidance services in this area remained a weak element in most countries.

Putting Policy into Practice in the United States In the US, different federal and state agencies—like the US Bureau of Labour Statistics, the Census Bureau, and the National Center for Education Statistics—have long been collecting large amounts of relevant data but they did this for different purposes, over different time periods, using different classifications. This made them hard to locate, to understand, and to use in relation to each other. The challenge was to integrate data from already existing sources into comprehensive and coherent occupational and career information systems for educators, counsellors, employment personnel, and vocational rehabilitation staff. To this end, in 1976 the US Congress created the National Occupational Information Coordinating Committee (called NOICC). To guarantee extension of the problem beyond the boundaries of politics, it created counterpart State Occupational Information Coordinating Committees (called SOICCs) in all the states and territories. Members of the National Committee represented no less than 10 different agencies in 5 federal departments. It signalled the start of an exemplary inter-agency, inter-state, and inter-departmental collaboration programme.

Public agencies, professional associations, and private vendors collaborated in developing systems and products. Federal seed money was matched by state and local funds to support and sustain information resources, delivery systems, and training. Information systems and products were tailored to the needs of a wide array of user groups. As a result of the collaboration and teamwork, most States are now delivering useful occupational and career information to their constituents.

More than 40 states offer access to computer-based career information delivery systems (CIDS) to millions of users annually. CIDS have become a major tool for career counsellors in many different settings across the United States and Canada. Training for information users. Occupational and career information may be essential but the NOICC/SOICC Network quickly learned that counsellors needed training if they were to use it effectively in their work. Therefore, as new information systems and products were introduced, their sponsors developed training programs in their use. SOICCs prepared guides to help teachers use career information newspapers in their classrooms. CIDS operators offered special training for counsellors using their systems.

Policies, partnerships, and strategies are needed to support career development. In the United States, the delivery of career information and counselling varies widely from state to state. Much depends on a particular state's policy, priorities and needs. On the whole, however, the public has greater access to career information and assistance because of the efforts of NOICC. The impetus for these improvements came from federal and state policies, expressed in legislation or funding. To implement these policies, the NOICC/SOICC Network employed six basic strategies:

— it focused on identifying and addressing its user needs;

— it used federal funds as seed money to leverage state and private funds. This supported the development of information systems, products, and training programs;

— It encouraged states to share innovative models and best practices—at national and regional conferences, in newsletters, and, more recently, via the Internet. Its online Library now offers a global repository for best practices in career development;

— It provided technical assistance and training. This enabled states to adapt and enhance successful models from other states;

— It built partnerships—first among federal and state agencies and later among public and private organisations. It tried to engage all stakeholders in its initiatives. This allowed it to draw on the expertise of professional leaders in designing and disseminating materials and training in their use;

— It emphasised training. Its strategy of training trainers gave its small network a much larger outreach to state and local constituents.

The way in which the EU is adapting information provision and training to the changed needs of the providers and users of career guidance and counselling is not unlike that of the US. However, the time-path is inevitably different, given the fact that close international collaboration in Europe is a more recent phenomenon than inter-state co-operation in the US. In fact, many of the integrating and facilitating processes described above are taking place at this very moment in time in the EU or are planned for the very near future. EU action in the area of guidance dates back to April 1963, when a Council Decision laid down the general principles for the implementation of a common vocational training policy. In it, career guidance was recognised as an important part of the learning process.

The Council recommended, among other things, the implementation of ongoing arrangements for vocational information, guidance and counselling for young people and adults, and ensuring that people would be able to use this system in good time before selecting a profession, whether during vocational training or at any other time in their lives. From there, a leap in time moves us on to 1990, when a Joint Opinion by the European Social Partners on the transition from school to adult and working life pulled guidance into the spotlights again by stressing its preventive role in heading off failure at school and dropping out, in balancing supply and demand for training, and in creating and strengthening links between training institutes and the world of business and industry. The vocational guidance strand of PETRA, an EU youth programme, aimed at promoting Community co-operation on guidance and at exchanging national facts and figures, good practice and effective methods for vocational guidance. Its objectives were to ensure that all young people receive appropriate information, practical guidance and interviews, as well as personal assistance to help them discover the occupational channels open to them, to assess their capacities and to encourage them to go for a vocational qualification and get into training.

As a result, today all young people and their families can get access to up-to-date information on the training opportunities and guidance services available in the other Member States, and they are encouraged and supported to use such information. The first phase of the Leonardo programme brought about the most recent innovations in systems, arrangements and actions. It covered a wide range of activities and tasks in connection with training and with the development of human resources in general.

Guidance and counselling have thus taken on a new and increasingly important role. Professional guidance services have a crucial role to play in the development of human resources. However, availability and quality of guidance services vary considerably. In none of them are all vulnerable sectors sufficiently covered yet. The offer of guidance is less developed for adults than for young people. It is therefore important for most countries to improve their guidance systems. In particular, increased efforts should be put into widening the recognition of guidance as an ongoing process which should start at school and continue ever thereafter. As guidance lies at the cross-roads between training, employment and personal development, it can provide a meeting place for the three types of professional currently operating separately in guidance: those linked to education and training systems, those linked to labour offices, and those providing guidance within companies.

5

Online Training for Counsellors

Despite the exponential advances in technology and the use of the World Wide Web in the field of education, finding ways to demonstrate and deliver services to students at all levels continues to be a challenge for counselor educators. Technological skills needed by human services professionals include a common core of skills needed by all educators and some skills unique to each discipline. School counselors in particular need technology skills to include knowledge of internet resources as well as knowing how to help students access them, guidance and counseling software, use of distance learning, use of listservs, and the interest to keep up to date on the ever changing scene of computer technology. Further, they need to learn to use technology for monitoring student progress and educational/career planning as well as to apply data to their professional decision making.

The use of online assignments in counselor education courses has been one way to teach and model the use of such technology for counselors in training.

Results and comments from students who have completed and applied such assignments to their work have been very positive. School counselors and counselor educators are increasingly recognizing the benefits of using technology in many areas of their jobs and of increasing their resources to help their students. Such technology can significantly alter the work of counselors in the areas of information retrieval and dissemination, college and career exploration, actual counseling interventions as well as in establishing networks of communication and support systems for clients. However, school counselors need to be more actively involved in actually implementing such technology into their jobs on a daily basis.

Recent studies have shown that many school counselors believe they have had inadequate training in using computers in their work. Therefore, it is essential to infuse such information, training, and knowledge of resources into their graduate education. To help students develop such competencies, a major emphasis needs to be placed on effective teaching and modeling by university faculty. Such technology and training can include the use of electronic mail and newsletters as a means of communication with students, parents and the community, learning about relevant websites, networking and implementing counseling strategies. Specific examples of applying such technology to counselor education can include accessing online legislative information relating to schools in general and counseling services specifically, using the internet to help students obtain information about higher education, sources of financial aid, career opportunities, and learning about mental health resources. Helping students develop websites to post their own work as well as list resources and activities for their students is another valuable skill to be learned.

Counselor educators are viewing applied technology as both a teaching tool and a necessary skill for their counselors in training. Acquiring technological skills is a developmental approach for counseling students who must be supported by counselor educators to move from "word processing to web pages to data analysis...". Counselor educators are in a position to have access to many resources to share with their students yet they realize that it is imperative to "shape" assignments or point students in specific directions to maximize the effectiveness of the assignments.

There is an ever increasing amount of information available on the internet and an essential skill for students to develop is not only to learn about the resources, but to learn how to apply the information gathered to their work in schools. There are growing numbers of counseling courses and programs offered online. And, there appears to be increasing external pressure from working students as well as internal pressure relating to budget issues within universities to provide on-line coursework. But there is also plenty of room for the use of "online" assignments within a more traditional graduate program. Giving such assignments within their classes has been a very effective way of helping their students learn about the content of specific websites and make significant applications of the information gleaned from the sites.

There are a variety of ways in which counselor educators can organize online instruction. Assignments may be done by individual course such as Career Development, Organization and Administration of the

Guidance and Counseling Program, Multicultural Counseling, or Counseling Theories. Another means of organization could be by topics that may be included within a particular course or may be infused throughout a number of courses. Examples of such topics could include, Legal and Ethical Issues in Counseling, Professional Organizations and Publications (such as ACA, ASCA, and ACES), and Resources for Counseling Children and Adolescents. A third example of organizing online assignments could be integrating them into counseling supervision. In a practicum or internship seminar students could be given assignments via electronic mail and could be organized into cyberspace forums where they could respond to each other's contributions. The weekly seminar would be an excellent opportunity for students and the university supervisor to share resources that have proved successful in their work and to collaborate on the development of a website that could be used with their students. Further, if internships are being conducted at a long distance from the university, online assignments and e-mail would be the primary way that professors and students communicate with one another.

There are a number of considerations to facilitate the smooth delivery of and maximize the opportunities for students in using online assignments. Counselor educators may decide to set up their own websites with resources organized and electronic addresses called universal resource locators (URL) listed for students. In this scenario, students can go to the instructor's website and click on the specific resources required for the assignment. An example of this format is used in the "Career Development" assignment given earlier. Another option is to spell out the URL for each task on the assignment and the student is responsible for typing them into the computer. A third option is for the instructor to give more general assignments in which the student is required to search and discover sites by topic or subject. In this last case, there is more room for variety and variability in the tasks given and responses made. Instructors who feel confident and are prepared to guide students through the process help students feel more comfortable in using the technology as part of their repertoire of skills. Such guidance is offered during the first part of the semester so that students can complete the assignment at their own pace and can use the resources offered as they need them.

It is essential that students understand the purpose of the assignment as well as how to use the computer in accessing the resources. Demonstrating the use of the Internet in general as well as specific websites is necessary. Including the online assignment as part of the course syllabus is another option for introducing the requirement early in the semester. Although the assignments may include some local as well as state and national resources, each instructor can adapt these assignments to the needs of their local student population. It is important for students to have a "product" as a result of the assignment. Simply asking students to go to a website does not ensure that they check it out or apply what they might find there. Having them answer questions about the site, or make comments/recommendations about the site, which are turned in to the instructor, is essential to the intent of the assignment. After all, once instructors have led students to the website, they want to be certain that students have not only "clicked" but have learned something from the experience. After the assignment is due, it can be useful to have students take turns coming to the front of the class and typing in their favorite URL to share with their classmates.

Computer-oriented Training Programs

Computers have been more widely used in counseling for record keeping, data analysis, cybercounseling and cyberlearning. In addition, counselor educators are beginning to use computer applications in the training of counselors. In US National Board for Certified Counselors (NBCC) and the Council for the Accreditation of Counseling and Related Educational Programs (CACREP) have adopted guidelines on the use of technology in training counselors. These progressive movements provide the impetus for incorporation of technology training in counselor preparation programs. The Association for Counselor Education and Supervision (ACES) Technology Interest Network recommended technical competencies necessary for counselor training. It recommend that at the completion of a counselor education program, students should:

— Be able to use productivity software to develop web pages, group presentations, letters, and reports.

— Be able to use such audiovisual equipment as video recorders, audio recorders, projection equipment, video conferencing equipment, and playback units.

— Be able to use computerized statistical packages.

— Be able to use computerized testing, diagnostic, and career decision-making programs with clients.

— Be able to use email.

— Be able to help clients search for various types of counseling-related information via the Internet, including information about careers, employment opportunities, educational & training opportunities, financial assistance/scholarships, treatment procedures, and social and personal information.

— Be able to subscribe, participate in, and sign off counseling related listservs.

— Be able to access and use counseling related CD-ROM databases.

These competencies are directly related to training counseling students and establish the first level of technology skills a counselor may need to be technologically competent. While computer competencies may be absolutes for counselors, many have not considered computer competencies involve a developmental process and require technical skills. Since 1984, the University of Iowa has incorporated an introductory computer course into the counselor education curriculum to expose masters' level students to computer technology. This course is designed to advance the use of technology for guidance and counseling professionals. The course emerged from a response from the school guidance and counseling professionals. The first course provided training in computer fundamentals on AppleIIw computers, using interactive video skills and CD-I, word processing, spreadsheet and database with AppleWorks, and graphics with MacPaint. The course has now expanded into teaching internet searching related to counseling, cybercounseling ethical responsibilities, development of web pages, presentation software and statistical packages. A distance hybrid learning approach is utilized by facilitating learning through web-based instruction called WebCT.

In US a study was designed to examine the lack of uniformity among counseling students. An investigation of the effectiveness of a required technology course on student computer competency appeared necessary. Research questions were as follows:

1. Do students with or without computer instruction differ significantly in computer competencies?
2. Do students with or without computer instruction differ significantly on their motivation towards computer usage?

The researchers hypothesized that students with computer instruction would differ from students without computer instruction on their level of computer competency and motivation towards computer usage.

The empirical study utilized a quasi-experimental cohort research design. This quasi-experimental design assumed quasi-comparability between successive cohorts. Therefore, the successive cohort groups were the summer and fall semester classes of 7C: 281 course at the University of Iowa. Comparisons were made between an experimental group and a control group. Pre and posttest scores were reported for the experimental group and compared to the pre-test scores of the control group. The statistical comparison was made between the summer (experimental group) posttest scores and the fall (control group) pre-test scores.

Twenty-six (experimental group N=16, control group N=10) masters level counseling students in the Division of Counseling, Rehabilitation, and Student Development were involved in the study. All students were enrolled in the 7C: 281 Introduction to Computers for Counselors course during the summer and fall semesters of 2001. The master's level students were in four counseling programs within the division: rehabilitation counseling, school counseling, student development, and substance abuse. Students voluntarily participated in the study.

The study participants consisted of 26 students with 84.2 % females and 15.8 % males. The respondents ranged in age from 22-57 years with 50% between 22-27 years old. Sixty-seven percent had a status of being a full-time student. Thirty-seven percent of the respondents were in the school counseling program, 32 % rehabilitation counseling program, 13 % substance abuse program, and 18% student development program. The mean number of courses completed toward a counseling degree was 6.1 with an average of 19.0 semester hours accumulated. Sixty-five percent indicated they had taken a technology course.

The experimental group consisted of 16 students with 89.3% females and 10.7% males. Forty-two percent of the respondents were in the school counseling program, 33% were in the rehabilitation counseling program, 18% were in the substance abuse counseling program, and 7% were in the student development program. These respondents ranged in age from 22-57 years.

The majority (43%) of the respondents were in the 22-27 age range with 36% aligning in the 28-33 years age range. The pretest surveys revealed 57% of experimental group respondents were full-time students and 68% had taken a computer course prior to this course. The mean number of courses completed toward a counseling degree was 5.3 with an average of 17.6 semester hours accumulated. Only one experimental group member reported that they had taken a course within the counselor education curriculum that utilized technology in the course.

The respondents were asked to identify the types of technology they currently used or have used previous to this course. Responses indicated 100% had used word processing software, 81% had used electronic mail, 50% had utilized audiovisual equipment, 44% had a course using web-based or web-assisted instruction, 18% acknowledged use of statistical programs, 18% cited usage of a listserv, 6% had used a cd-rom, and 6% indicated other technology. The posttest survey was completed by only 12 of the 16 original respondents. Two respondents specified they had taken a course within counselor education curriculum that utilized technology. Respondents were asked to identify the types of technology they currently used or had used before the technology course. These responses yielded the following frequency information on usage was provided: 96% word processing software, 89% electronic mail, 53% audiovisual equipment, 54% web-based or web-assisted instruction, 32% statistical software, 25% listserv, 14% cd-roms, and 7% other technology.

The control group consisted of 10 masters students enrolled in the 7C: 281 Introduction to Computers For Counselors course. The control group consisted of 60.0% females and 40.0% males. Fifty percent of the respondents were in the student development program, 30% were in rehabilitation counseling program, and 20% were in the school counseling program. These respondents ranged in age from 21-33 years.

The majority (70%) of the respondents were in the 22-27 age range. Eighty percent were full-time students and 70% had taken a computer course prior to this class.

The average number of courses taken toward completion of a counseling degree was 5.6 with a mean cumulative semester hours score of 15.8. Two respondents from the control group reported they had taken a counseling course, which required the use of technology. Respondents were asked to identify the types of technology experience they held prior to the technology course. Their responses indicated usage in the following areas: 100% word processing software, 100% electronic mail, 60% audiovisual equipment, 60% web-based or web-assisted instruction, 10% statistical software, 60% listservs, 3% cd-roms, and 1% other technology.

Prospective participants were master's level counselor education students at The University of Iowa in the College of Education enrolled in the 7C: 281 Introduction to Computers in Counseling one-hour semester course. The students were given a cover letter introducing the research study, a survey and an informed consent document for voluntary participation in the study during the first class session. Students could choose not to participate by checking no on the informed consent document and returning the uncompleted surveys. Completed surveys to be given to the researchers were placed in an envelope. The informed consent documents were placed in a separate envelope to maintain the anonymity of the participants. Students were given the same survey again at the end of the semester as a posttest survey.

Demographic information. Students were asked to provide the following demographic information: gender, age, degree program, computer courses taken, degree of computer skills, types of courses completed, courses taken that integrated web-based or web-assisted instruction, types of technologies used, number of courses completed toward degree, and number of semester hours completed. Surveys were coded based on whether they were pre or post-test instruments.

Computer Technology Competencies Scale (CTCS). The CTCS was created using 12 competency areas recommended by the ACES Technology Interest Network and developed 15 items to measure an individual's competence level on the technology competency. A 5-point Likert scale was developed, ranging from 1 (not familiar) to 5 (very confident). Participants were instructed to indicate their competence level on each of 15 computer technology items. The initial reliability data revealed good internal consistency, with a with Cronbach's alpha of a =. 93. Validity data for CTCS are not available.

Situational Motivation Scale (*SIMS*). This 20-item Situational Motivation scale consists of five subscales with four questions designed to assess situational variables that affect the experience of intrinsic motivation, extrinsic motivation, and amotivation. Extrinsic motivation was identified through two extrinsic motivational subscales of identified regulation and external regulation. Intrinsic motivation was identified through one intrinsic motivational subscale. Amotivation was identified through one amotivation subscale. The measure of introjected regulation was developed by borrowing from a previously validated questionnaire. The items from the RTWS were adapted specifically for the study. The adapted items used precise experiences in distance education obtained from a literature review of self-determination.

The SIMS scale uses the response stem (e.g., "Why are you currently participating in distance education?" or

"Why are you currently not participating in distance education?"), with a 1 to 7 Likert response scale (strongly disagree, disagree, somewhat disagree, neutral, somewhat agree, agree, strongly agree) for each of the 20 items. Totals for each subscale were computed by averaging the relevant four items. Guay et al. reported the construct validity and assessed it by two correlation analyses. Their results found an overall pattern of interrelations among the subscales is formed from an ordered pattern of those subscales adjacent along the continuum. For example, intrinsic motivation correlated positively with identified regulation (r =. 36) but negatively with amotivation (r = -.41). The second correlation analysis was performed between the SIMS subscales and perceived competence and concentration/behavioral intentions. There was a strong positive correlation (SIMS subscales with motivational determinant and consequences) observed with intrinsic motivation and identified regulation but a strong negative correlation with amotivation and external regulation. These correlations were consistent with those predicted by self-determination theory. The subscales' internal consistency values or Cronbach Alphas were: intrinsic motivation a =.92, identified regulation a =.80, external regulation a =.86, and amotivation a =.77.

Prior to analysis, variables were examined for accuracy of data entry, missing values, and fit between their distributions. During data entry, precautions were taken to ensure there was no human error in the data entry process. The precaution procedures were to pull out every third questionnaire and check to see if the data entered into SPSS were correct. All analyses were performed using SPSS 9.0 to provide descriptive statistics. Internal consistency for the two scales used in the study was explored by calculating alpha coefficients of reliability for the total score of each scale as well as SIMS subscales. Frequencies and means were calculated for all demographic characteristics of the sample. In keeping with the cohort design, the statistical hypotheses were that the mean scores of the experimental group pretest did differ from those of the experimental group posttest scores on the CTCS. A one-way analysis of variance was performed to test this hypothesis. The CTCS scale items were computed by averaging items.

The dependent variables were CTCS averaged score. The independent variable in the research was time when the test was taken (pretest or posttest). The results revealed that computer competency was increased after taking the introductory computer course. The results of the analysis of variance revealed that the experimental group differed significantly from the control group on the Computer Technology Competency Scale (F (1, 20) = 7.519, p =.013). Examination of the group means revealed a significant difference in mean scores between the experimental group (M =3.60) and control group (M = 2.71) on computer competencies. This result demonstrates an increase in computer competency after completing the required introduction to computers in counseling course. The results of the t-test revealed that several items on the CTCS scale yielded a significant difference between the experimental and control groups: ethics (t[19] = 4.254, p=.000), assisting client with internet searches (t[19] = 2.199, p=.040), statistical package (t[20] = 5.520, p=.000), listserv (t[19] = 2.705, p=.014), cd-rom (t[19] = 2.827, p=.011), presentation software (t[20] = 2.237, p=.037), and evaluating information from the internet (t[20] = 2.359, p=.029).

The group means indicate that the experimental group increased computer competency after completing the course under the following competency items: ethics (M=4.00), assisting clients with Internet searches (M=3.00), statistical software (M=2.92), listserv (M=2.91), cd-rom (M=3.00), presentation software (M=4.17), and evaluating information from the internet (M=3.92). The group means from the control group indicated computer competency were low before the computer course was taken under the following competency items: ethics (M=2.00), assisting clients with Internet searches (M=1.70), statistical software (M=1.10), listserv (M=1.60), cd-rom (M=1.60), presentation software (M=3.00), and evaluating information from the internet (M=2.70). The results of the analysis of variance revealed that the experimental group pretest and posttest results differed significantly on the Computer Technology Competency Scale (F (1, 26) = 38.007, p =.000). Examination of the group means revealed a significant difference in mean scores between the post-test scores (M =3.60) and pre-test scores (M = 1.97) on computer competencies. This result demonstrates an increase in computer competency after completing the required introduction to computers in counseling course.

The results of the analysis of variance revealed that all the items with the exception of word processing on the CTCS scale yielded a significant difference between the posttest and pretest: word processing (F (1, 26) = 1.438, p =.241, email (F (1, 26) = 4.508, p =.043), bulletin board (F (1, 26) = 12.118, p =.002), knowledge of ethics Internet (F (1, 26) = 29.630, p =.000), computerized testing (F (1, 26) = 12.306, p =.000), assisting clients with Internet (F (1, 26) = 11.045, p =.003), statistical packages (F (1, 26) = 39.918, p =.000), Internet for research (F (1, 25) = 9.580, p =.005), counseling listservs (F (1, 25) = 7.080, p =.013), Internet for continuing education (F (1, 25) = 15.558, p

=.001), counseling CD-Rom (F (1, 25) = 14.103, p =.001), database (F (1, 26) = 13.180, p =.001), presentation software (F (1, 26) = 36.322, p =.000), developing web pages (F (1, 26) = 59.313, p =.000), and evaluate the quality of information provided via Internet (F (1, 26) = 30.128, p =.000).

Group means indicate the experimental group posttest results significant increase in their computer competency after completing the course in under the following competency items: ethics posttest (M=4.00), ethics pretest (M=2.0), computerized testing pretest M=1.56), computerized testing posttest (M=3.0), assisting clients with Internet searches pretest (M=1.50), assisting clients with Internet searches posttest (M=2.82), statistical software pretest (M=1.19), statistical software posttest (M=2.92), listserv posttest (M=1.50), listserv pretest (M=2.91), cd-rom pretest (M=1.50), cd-rom posttest (M=3.00), presentation software pretest (M=1.75), presentation software posttest (M=4.17), evaluating information from the internet posttest (M=1.88), and evaluating information from the internet posttest (M=3.92). Results that measure motivation towards computers revealed no group differences existed on motivation factors of participants in the study on external regulation, identified regulation (value toward computers), introjected regulation (participating because of guilt), amotivation (indifferent), intrinsic. Thus, indicating motivation toward computer usage may not be a factor in training.

Findings from the study support the research hypothesis that students will increase their computer competency based on completing a computer course. Both the experimental group (EG) and the control group (CG) yielded lower mean scores on some of the competency areas indicating the need for further research and instruction. These competency areas included: assisting clients with Internet searches (EG, M=2.82; CG, M=1.70), statistical packages (EG, M=2.92; CG, M=1.10), listserv (EG, M=2.91; CG, M=1.60), and cd-rom (EG, M=3.00; CG, M=1.60). The experimental group pretest and posttest results showed significant difference among all the items on CTCS with the exception of word processing. Therefore, student competency areas were low on all the items In the study both the experimental and control groups demonstrated similar levels of motivation to participate in computer technology as indicated by scores on the SIMS motivational scale. Thus, they were not hindered in participating in computer technology. However, the course appears to help students improve skills on some of the computer competencies. Areas such as, being familiar with statistical packages, assisting clients in internet searches, and knowledge of listservs need an increase in competency level.

Implications for counselors are tempered by considerations of threats to validity.

First, external validity is threatened by the restricted nature of the sample and the purposive sampling strategy.

Second, the multiple t-tests increase the probability of Type 1 error.

Third, the institutional cohort design, by its nature, is relatively a weak quasi-experimental design and leaves open some threat to internal validity, especially history.

Fourth, the pretest of the experimental group added an additional threat to internal validity. Although these threats to validity do limit the applicability of these results, they are partially allayed by the consistency of the previous studies using this design.

Computer competency increases with exposure to computer technology in a required introductory course. Application of computer technology to practice cannot be assumed, it must be taught. The application of computer technology is normally taught through performance assessment. Students are taught how to operate and demonstrate different software and equipment by producing several assignments for the course. These assignments can be graded as pass/fail. This may benefit the student by allowing them to learn programs without feeling pressure to receive letter grades. This also allows the instructor to discuss possible problem-solving techniques to help the student make connections between computer technology principles and professional practice decisions.

Finally, an introductory course, which discusses technology integration into counseling courses in the program, aids with future instruction for faculty because instructional time for technology is not used in the regular courses.

Development of Standards

The tremendous growth of technology led to standards being developed to impact the university training programs of both counselors and educators. School counseling programs are thus being impacted by technology developments and standards in both the fields of counseling and education and faced with the challenge of creating competencies that meet the technology issues and needs in both arenas. While the roots of computer assisted counselor training can be traced back to Wizenbaum's ELIZA in the mid 1960's, it was not until the 1990's that technology was truly recognized as a force impacting both the education and practice of counselors. Since the mid 1990's, technology in counseling has been the focus of numerous articles, chapters, and books.

Technology itself has become a medium through which information and scholarly publication on the use of technology in counseling is disseminated. Online libraries and CD-ROM databases carry full text journal articles. Electronic journals listed by the State Library of Colorado which specifically deal with technology in counseling, education, or psychology currently numbers 37. Listservs, email-based discussion groups, like the International Counseling Network (ICN) and the Counselor Education and Supervision Network-List (CESNET-L), while not specifically devoted to technology in counseling, often contain information related to its use in both training and practice. Along with the tremendous growth of technology in the field of counseling, professional organizations have seen the need for standards around its use.

The US National Board for Certified Counselors (1997) saw the impact that on-line technology was beginning to have upon the field of counseling and developed "The Practice of Internet Counseling". The National Career Development Association created "Guidelines for the Use of the Internet for Provision of Career Information and Planning Services" and, while the International Association of Educational and Vocational Guidance does not have ethical guidelines specific to the use of technology, their General Assembly, in the

"Declaration of Counsellor Qualification Standards", declared "an urgent need for internationally recognised qualification standards for counsellors, and ... [established] a committee consisting of members from different regions in the world to elaborate a draft of such standards."

Additionally, the Association for Counselor Education and Supervision (ACES), believing that the effective use of technology was a crucial skill for counselors, created a Technology Interest Network. The members of this network developed "Technical Competencies for Counselor Education Students: Recommended Guidelines For Program Development" which was endorsed by the ACES Executive Council. Even with these ethical and skill guidelines, the concern regarding the use of technology is so great that some continue to call for an expansion of the ethical guidelines and the creation of comprehensive standards for counseling related web sites.

While technology was coming into its own in the counseling field, it was virtually exploding into the field of education. In US throughout their eight years in office, the Clinton-Gore Administration made an unprecedented commitment to bring technology into the Pre-K-12 classroom. The Congress approved billions of dollars to provide teachers with training and support, develop effective software and online learning resources, provide access to computers, and connect every school to the Internet. The FY01 budget for the Education Office of Educational Technology alone provides $958 million for education technology and research. Additionally, private industry, such as Microsoft, Intel, Hewlett Packard; and foundations, such as the Bill and Linda Gates Foundation, and Verizon Foundation, have given billions of dollars to help schools and teachers obtain equipment and the professional development necessary to effectively integrate technology into the curriculum. National professional education organizations have developed technology standards. The International Society for Technology in Education, through the National Educational Technology Standards Project (NETS), created Standards for Students, NETS for Teachers, and is currently working on NETS for School Administrators. In US as the national scene was becoming filled with technology stakeholders, state legislatures and departments of education began to see the importance of technology in education as well.

In response to the demand for technology proficient educators, the National Council for the Accreditation of Teacher Education (NCATE) formed a Task Force on Technology and Teacher Education in 1996. This group studied the impact of technology upon education and the ensuing need for teacher education programs to integrate technology education into their pre-service training programs. Their report, "Technology and the New Professional Teacher: Preparing for the 21st Century Classroom", described the skills needed by educators to help students.

In US, the field of school counseling has been affected by the impact technology has had in both counseling and Pre-K-12 education. The Elementary School Guidance & Counseling journal published a special issue devoted to technology in school counseling in October 1995. In early 1999, as part of its Transforming School Counseling Implementation Grant, Indiana State University's (ISU) School Counselor Program began to seriously look at the specific technology skills that school counseling students should be able to perform by the time they have completed their two year masters degree program. In addition to studying the skill sets developed by ACES and Hartman, focus groups were conducted with area school counselors.

A careful review of the current and emerging trends in technology in both education and counseling was carried out in order to ascertain their possible impact upon the field of school counseling. Finally, ISU's own School Counselor Student Competencies were examined to see what technology skills would help students in the acquisition and performance of these proficiencies. The resulting 10 competencies became the School Counseling Program Technology Proficiencies, which are as follows:

— Be a knowledgeable consumer and skilled, effective, and efficient user of computers, technology, and the Internet. Understanding and being skilled in technology does not necessarily mean knowing how to effectively and efficiently use it. For example, unless school counselors know how to efficiently search the World Wide Web, a search for information on Attention Deficit Hyperactive Disorder will yield tens of thousands of "hits" and take hours of time searching for helpful and reliable information geared to a particular user, be it a student, teacher, parent, or the counselor. Additionally, once resources are found, school counselors must know how to evaluate the validity and applicability of its content.

— Be a knowledgeable and effective teacher and facilitator for teachers, students and parents concerning educational and career technology resources. School counselors must not only be proficient users of technology-related educational and career development resources, they must also be able to show students, parents, and educators how to effectively use these resources.

— Be familiar with trends in the use of technology in education and their impact upon student academic achievement levels and social, educational, and career development; and, intelligently contribute to the development of a school wide technology plan. Technology can positively or negatively affect not only a student's academic development, but their personal, educational, and/or career development as well. School counselors have the responsibility to understand the possible impact of technology upon student development and to advocate on behalf of their best interests.

— Be able to use a wide variety of technology resources, including Internet tools, appropriate software, and digit cameras, in the development, implementation, and evaluation of counseling and guidance activities. Based upon a sound understanding of the impact of technology upon development and academic achievement, school counselors must be able to effectively incorporate technology into their developmental guidance programs. This would include the development of student competencies that would include the use of technology in areas like study skills and career exploration.

— Be able to develop short and long-term technology plans for the counseling department that provide students and families access to guidance and counseling services, and, articulate the opportunities, as well as the ethical and legal implications of technology as a counseling and guidance delivery tool. When designing a comprehensive developmental guidance program, school counselors must think not only about staffing and facility needs, but also realize that the purposeful acquisition and intentional deployment of technology is an integral component of the plan. Technology should not be just a program add on. It should be seamlessly, yet deliberately, infused within the program's infrastructure.

— Be able to design, create, and evaluate an effective, interactive Internet site for a counseling and guidance program. A school's counseling program Internet site becomes a virtual office where students, families, teachers, area employers, etc. can gain information, submit forms, have discussions and participate in activities and projects. School counselors need to know how to design, create and evaluate effective sites, being mindful of the ethical issues and standards.

— Objectively evaluate counseling and guidance software and articulate software needs and plans to school technology professionals and commercial vendors. Schools will look to their counselors for direction in purchasing counseling and guidance related software. Therefore, school counselors must be able to objectively and competently evaluate the match between the objectives of the software purchase and the features of the reviewed software.

— Understand the ethical and legal implications of technology, including issues of equity and access and the implications of the digital divide upon students, families, and communities. While skill in the use of technology is important, school counselors have the responsibility to understand the ethical and legal issues which surround the use of technology. Additionally, they must understand ramifications inherent in the digital divide. All decisions concerning technology use must be predicated upon these considerations.

— Effectively use technology, including relational databases, spreadsheets and the Internet, that allows the analysis of student achievement and related data; and, how to use technology to support the change needed to raise student achievement levels. It is important for school counselors to know how to effectively and efficiently uses technology to monitor student achievement, from the individual student and classroom levels to the whole grade and school levels. Being able to effectively use technology in data analysis, to spur change in classrooms, and to facilitate whole school reform is especially important with education's current focus upon high standards and accountability.

— Effectively use technology as a tool in advocacy efforts and the procurement of funds and resources. Finally, technology can be an extremely effective tool in the advocacy efforts of school counselors. Whether it is used in the creation of a school board presentation with charts and graphs from presentation software, or in finding grant opportunities on the World Wide Web, technology is an important means to the furtherance of advocacy endeavors.

6

Psychological Problems of Netizens

The virtual world is quite different than the in-person world. Digitizing people, relationships, and groups has stretched the boundaries of how and when humans can interact. In different online environments we see different combinations of these features, thus resulting in a distinct psychological quality to each environment which determines how people experience themselves and others. These features as the fundamenal elements of a conceptual model for a psychology of cyberspace. In fact, the effect of these elements on individuals, groups, and communities is an important theme throughout this book.

Whether an environment in cyberspace involves visual and/or auditory communication will greatly affect how people behave and the relationships that develop among people. The multimedia chat environments, audio-video conferencing, and internet-phoning surely are signs of things to come. However, the sensory experience of encountering others in cyberspace - seeing, hearing, and combining seeing and hearing - is still limited. For the most part people communicate through typed language. Even when audio-video conferencing becomes efficient and easy to use, people will probably never be able to physically interact with each other - no handshakes, pats on the back, hugs, or kisses.

The limited sensory experiences of cyberspace has some significant disadvantages - as well as some unique advantages - as compared to in-person encounters. E-mail, chat, and instant messaging continue to be the most common forms of online interaction for reasons beyond their ease of use and inexpense compared to multimedia tools.

Drawing on different cognitive abilities than talking and listening, typing one's thoughts and reading those of another is a unique way to present one's identity, perceive the identity of one's online companion, and establish a relationship. E-mail relationships in particular have evolved into a very complex, text-based process - with chat or IM relationships approaching that complexity.

The lack of face-to-face cues has a curious impact on how people present their identity in cyberspace. Communicating only with typed text, you have the option of being yourself, expressing only parts of your identity, assuming imaginative identities, or remaining completely anonymous - in some cases, being almost invisible, as with the "lurker." The multimedia worlds also offer the opportunity to express yourself through the visual costumes known as "avatars." Anonymity has a disinhibiting effect that cuts two ways. Sometimes people use it to act out some unpleasant need or emotion, often by abusing other people. Or it allows them to be honest and open about some personal issue that they could not discuss in a face-to-face encounter.

While reading e-mail or text talk in chat rooms, some people experience a blending of their mind with that of the other person. In the imaginary multimedia worlds - where people shape-shift, speak via ESP, walk through walls, and spontaneously generate objects out of thin air - the experience becomes surrealistic. It mimics a state of consciousness that resembles dreams. These altered and dream-like states of consciousness in cyberspace may account for why it is so attractive for some people. It might help explain some forms of computer and cyberspace addiction.

In most cases, everyone on the internet has an equal opportunity to voice him or herself. Everyone - regardless of status, wealth, race, gender, etc. - starts off on a level playing field. Some people call this the "net democracy." Although one's status in the outside world ultimately will have some impact on one's life in cyberspace, there is some truth to this net democracy ideal.

Geographical distance makes little difference in who can communicate with whom. An engineer in Germany converses with a business woman from California on a server in Australia. It's a small world after all. The irrelevance of geography has important implications for people with unique interests or needs.

In their outside life, they may not be able to find anyone near them who shares that unique interest or need. But in cyberspace, birds of a feather - even those with highly unusual feathers - easily can flock together. For support groups devoted to helping people with their problems, that can be a very beneficial feature of cyberspace. For people with antisocial motivations, that's a very negative feature of cyberspace.

"Synchronous communication" involves people sitting at their computer at the same time (i.e., in "real time") communicating with each other via the internet. Chat rooms are one example. On the other hand, e-mail and newsgroups involve "asynchronous communication" that does not require people to interact with each other in the moment.

In both asynchronous and synchronous communication (with the exception of video conferencing and internet phoning), there is a stretching of time. During chat you have from several seconds to a minute or more to reply to the other person - a significantly longer delay than in face-to-face meetings. In e-mail or newsgroups, you have hours, days, or even weeks to respond.

Cyberspace creates a unique temporal space where the ongoing, interactive time together stretches out. This provides a convenient "zone for reflection." Compared to face-to-face encounters, you have significantly more time to mull things over and compose a reply. Some new internet users go through a period of adaptation to this novel temporal experience.

For example, they may expect a reply to their e-mail immediately. Enthused about e-mail relating, they assume (perhaps unconsciously) that their partner's reply will approximate the rate of an in-person conversation. Experienced e-mail users appreciate the advantages of time stretching, and even come to understand that different e-mail users have their own e-mail pace. In other ways, cyberspace time is condensed. If you are a member of an online community for several months, you may be considered an "old-timer."

Internet environments change rapidly because it's a lot easier to write and rewrite software infrastructure than it is to build with bricks, wood, and iron. Because it's easy to move around cyberspace, who we meet and the membership of online groups also changes rapidly. By posting a message on bulletin boards read by countless numbers of users, people can draw to themselves others who match even their most esoteric interests. Using a web search engine, they can scan through millions of pages in order to zoom their attention onto particular people and groups. The internet will get more powerful as tools for searching, filtering, and contacting specific people and groups become more effective.

The ability to sift through so many online possibilities for developing relationships amplifies an interesting interpersonal phenomenon well-known to psychologists. A user will act on unconscious motivations - as well as conscious preferences and choices - in selecting friends, lovers, and enemies. This "transference" guides towards specific types of people who address our underlying emotions and needs. Pressed by hidden expectations, wishes, and fears, this unconscious filtering mechanism has at its disposal an almost infinite candy store of online alternatives to choose from.

Most online activities, including e-mail correspondence and chat sessions, can be recorded and saved to a computer file. Unlike real world interactions, the user in cyberspace can keep a permanent record of what was said, to whom, and when. Because these interactions are purely document-based, we may even go so far as to say that the relationship between people are the documents, and that the relationship can be permanently recorded in its entirety.

These records may come in very handy to the user. You can reexperience and reevaluate any portion of the relationship you wish. You can use quoted text as feedback to the partner. One sign of a flame war is the blossoming of the infamous arrows >> that highlight the ammunition of quoted text. Although it's tempting to think of the saved text as an objective record of some piece of the relationship, it's fascinating to see how different your emotional reactions to the same exact record can be when you reread it at different times.

The beauty of computer simulated environments is their ability to transform reality as we know it. They do not have to recreate the actual world. Instead, they can construct imaginary environments, fantasy realms where the usual laws of reality are stretched, altered, or negated.

You walk through walls, communicate telepathically, live out a scene from a movie or book, do anything your imagination can conjure up in any surrounding of your choice. It can be a dream-like experience, if that's what you want. Perhaps the term "virtual reality" applies to these environments in the sense that the imaginary experience could feel AS IF it was real. Fantasy becomes reality. It's important to note that the magnitude of these imaginary features could be controlled.

Some scenarios might involve only a sprinkling of fantasy - like a walk to the top of the Eiffel Tower, where you eat lunch at your favorite cafe that has been transported intact from New York City. Other scenes could be intensely imaginative. Like being a flock of birds that dissolves into wispy clouds above the Grand Canyon.

A problem with imaginary environments will be disorientation and sensory overstimulation. Nature shaped the human perceptual system to work efficiently within specific parameters. Designing fantasy environments for a person must take into consideration that person's biologically predetermined limits for sensory stimulation.

Other problematic reactions to imaginary scenarios will involve more complex psychological factors. Alterations in one's virtual body could trigger dissociation, identity diffusion and disruption, or disintegration anxiety. It will be important to assess the appropriate fantasy scene for any given person. From a research perspective, experimenting with imaginative environments can help psychology better understand the parameters of human sensation, perception, and identity construction.

Using current multimedia chat software, some people prefer the third person view of their avatars interacting in a visual scene (e.g., Palace), rather than the more claustrophobic, "head-in-a-box" feeling of first person scenes. Once technology gives users more peripheral vision, that closed-in feeling may be less of a problem. Yet some people may still prefer the feeling of objectivity and even transcendence that third person views offer.

A powerful virtual reality will offer both options - to immerse and to step out and view the scenario from a distance. In "real" life, wouldn't it be very helpful to step out of a situation you're in so you can examine it from a safer, more objective distance? In virtual reality - especially scenarios that are especially arousing or disorienting - the ability to process the scene from a third person view might be very useful. Psychologists call it an "observing ego."

Ultimately, all dichotomies are more a conceptual convenience than an absolute truth. It's probably more accurate to think of true-to-life and imaginary VRs as opposite poles on a continuum. In between, there are varying mixtures of reality and fantasy - some more reality-rich, others more fantasy-rich. There is at least one other way that the two paths of VR weave in and out of each other. Any fantasy has its roots in the unconscious - in hidden wishes, fears, and needs.

Psychological Issues of Cyberworld

The new technology comes in the form of an international computing/telecommunications network known as the internet, and it may potentially have as significant an impact upon human culture as did the invention of the printing press. The precursor to the internet was created in 1969 by an arm of the Defense Department called the Defense Advanced Research Program Agency (DARPA).

This computer network, which eventually came to be known as Arpanet, was primarily designed as a means for Defense-sponsered researchers to operate different computers at a distance; the computer conferencing capabilities and subsequent social aspects of the network emerged as a byproduct of its operation. The network was purposefully intended to be decentralized so that, in the event of a nuclear attack, it would be practically impossible to shut down. Initially there were only four sites connected via the network. By 1971 there were about 24, and by 1981 there were more than 200 sites online. Today it is estimated that there are over 30 million people connected to the internet, with usage increasing approximately 10% per month, and the number of new applications and services growing almost as quickly. Along with this explosion there is emerging a new set of subcultural phenomena which is loosely referred to as cyberculture. Though some research has been conducted concerning the nature of this emergent culture, the main stream of social scientists has paid it little attention, or failed to notice its arrival altogether.

Most of the existing literature centers on issues pertaining to computer conferencing. However, computer conferencing is merely one aspect of computer mediated communication (CMC). One such neglected domain of CMC, though argued by some to be the most indicative of cyberculture is that known as the Multi-User Dimension (MUD). A MUD is a network-accessable, multi-participant, user-extensible virtual reality which is primarily text-based.

Typically, the term "virtual reality" refers to computer simulated environments which possess varying degrees of audio/visual interface, and although some experimental MUDs do offer AV components, this form of virtual reality is essentially text-based. The name "MUD" first appeared in 1978 when a student named Roy Trubshaw at the University of Essex, England, created a program that he called a "Multi-User Dungeon".

It was a multi-user adventure game loosely based upon the popular game known as "Dungeons and Dragons". In this fantasy adventure, players were encouraged to compete with each other for points by going on quests to slay monsters or find treasure.

All players started out on an equal footing, but after having accumulated a certain number of points a player could advance his rank, thus granting him access to new and greater powers. This eventually lead to a sort of social hierarchy which spanned from "Newbies" though various intermediate levels, and culminating in attainment of the title "Wizard", with all the special powers and privileges of such rank.

From this fantasy-adventure based beginning, MUDs have since proliferated and diversified so that at present one can find hundreds of MUDs throughout the internet, many of which have been put to uses other than merely recreation. To reflect this evolution, the acronym MUD has come to stand for Multi-User Dimension or Multi-User Domain as well as the original Multi-User Dungeon.

Additionally, the term MUD has recently differentiated into various sub-types such as MOO, MUSH, MUSE, MUCK, DUM, etc. Each of these acronyms is intended to indicate, though with quite a degree of overlap, the multiple environmental conditions and purposes of each community. One virtual space, created by Amy Bruckman of the Massachusetts Institute of Technology Media Lab, is called the MediaMOO (MOO designating MUD-Object Oriented). This environment provides a virtual meeting place for students and academics working in the area of media and communications.

Community members are encouraged to build onto this virtual world by creating new objects, rooms, and features via a MOO programming language.

It is generally speculated that computers and computer networks will transform (are transforming) the ways in which society functions. These changes are occurring on multiple levels, effecting our modes of production, our modes of learning, and even the ways in which we socialize. There is even evidence to suggest that use of interactive multimedia actually alters ones neurological configuration, and a preliminary draft of the DSM-V includes a section delineating newly emerging "Cyber Disorders".

MUD characters have no actuality, only virtuality. They are never immutable. MUD characters are not fixed, and they are always in the process of redefinition. They are cyborgs - entities made up of ones and zeroes and imagination, without bodies and without physical restrictions in the virtuality they inhabit.

The objects in MUD universes are treated as if they had the properties of the everyday counterparts. Houses are lived in, roses are smelt, food can be eaten and other players can be kissed. Such technology is a device which mediates between the physical and the imagined. It is an interface between the imagined world and the world of the body. It is in the spaces between the body and the self that cyborgs exists.

In the real-world one does have to contend with different types of social and environmental conditions to an extent, but at least one can be fairly certain of a multitude of constants (for instance, there are no dragons in the real-world and the laws of gravity are always in effect). In a MUD it is literally true that "reality" is created through language both by the actions of the players and through the code used by the programmers.

One study demonstrated that both the types and frequency of graphic accents correlated with player gender, with men being less prone to utilize such devices than women. However, it did not appear that there was a significant difference in the rate or degree of flaming. This tendency for women to be more challenging in CMC groups as compared to face-to-face interactions may be due to women feeling more at ease in CMC because of the relative anonymity, or that it may be that the women engaged in CMC might already be involved in male-dominated endeavors such as high tech. organizations or academia.

Since MU* interaction is essentially synchronous, these findings have to be considered with this distinction in mind. One factor that complicates gender related research in such environments is that, due to the anonymity of the medium, one can never be certain of the sex of a respondent. Gender switching has been documented by other researchers as well.

An interesting finding is that the vast majority of those adopting opposite genders seem to be men; women rarely report such behavior. Of the women that did admit to interacting as opposite gender characters, many of them expressed shock at what was perceived as an abrupt drop in the degree and frequency of helpful gestures and general civility offered by other "male" characters.

Conversely, men consistently reported that their female characters received more assistance and generally prospered better than did their alternate male characters. It should be noted however, that information gathered through on-line interviews may not be wholly reliable due to the very fact that one can never be absolutely certain of the true gender of the respondent. Indeed, any self-reports stemming from such an inherently fantasy laden construct must be accepted with a degree of skepticism.

There have even been reports of Internet related deaths, such as cardiac arrests resulting from sleep deprivation and lack of personal maintenance or suicides due to Net related stress. Such obsessive behavior has become quite a problem on some college campuses where computer facility administrators have had to literally "pull the plug" on some addicted students.

In fact, MUDing has been outlawed on the continent of Australia because of the excessive satellite link-up costs associated with such activities. Little is known about this new form of addiction, but as mentioned previously a preliminary draft of the DSM-V includes a section delineating some of these types of "Cyber Disorders". People may be friendlier towards one another in cyberspace.

A recent survey of public school teachers who utilize the Internet as a classroom resource revealed that, except for its function as an information archive, "the rewarding social atmosphere" was viewed as the most outstanding feature of Net access.

Likewise, studies conducted in educational settings where internet access is available have revealed that children are less critical of differences via CMC than in face to face groups. Additionally, a study by Masinter & Ostram on the effectiveness of multi-user information retrieval systems revealed that peer collaboration is higher in on-line information access than it is in "physical" libraries.

Yet a study of electronic bulletin boards conducted at Temple University revealed that Internet groups seem to form, interact and go through distinct stages just as do "real-life" groups, implying that virtual groups may only seem to be more cooperative, friendly, etc.. Likewise,

Kiesler et al, in one of the first studies ever conducted on Net related psychological phenomena, concluded that not only did computer mediated communication impede a group's ability to reach a consensus, but that it was practically devoid of the types of nonverbal social cues necessary to sustain the type of social climate Resnick claims is inherent in the medium.

The perception of friendliness may also be confounded by the temperament of the individuals under study as it relates to computer environments in general. For example, it seems plausible that those who are somewhat technophobic might find any form of CMC to be unfriendly, whereas individuals that embrace technology might perceive the same environment as warm and inviting.

Psychological dynamics of Online Conversations

The word "chat" surely connotes a superficial mode of relating. Indeed, conversation in a chat room often is less than "deep." But as we've seen in the log excerpts so far, the conversation sometimes is very meaningful. Despite the staccato style and the potential for buzzing confusion, discussions can be very fluid, sophisticated, and personal. In the beginning, there was TextTalk. And only TextTalk. But even with the advent of video and audio streaming, typed text continues to reign supreme as the primary mode of conversing on the internet.

This is especially true of "synchronous" modes of communication, as in the ever-popular IRC channels and chat rooms of AOL. Even in the multimedia chat communities, like Palace, where users communicate with avatars and sounds within a visual backdrop, typed text remains the front line method of "talking." TextTalk in online chat environments has evolved into a fascinating style of communication. In some ways, it is strikingly similar to face-to-face (ftf) dialogue.

In other ways, it is quite unique. Many of its unique qualities revolve around the fact that it is an austere mode of communication. There are no changes in voice, no facial expressions, no body language, no (or very little) visual/spatial environment as a context of meaning. There's just typed words. Some people find that experience too sparse. They feel disoriented, disembodied, adrift in that screen of silently scrolling dialogue.

Other people love the minimalist style of TextTalk. They love to see how people creatively express themselves despite the limitations. They love to immerse themselves in the quiet flow of words that feels like a more direct, intimate connection between one's mind and the minds of others. Almost as if the other is inside one's head. Almost as if you are talking with a part of yourself. Without the distracting sights and sounds of the ftf world, TextTalk feels like a more pure communication of ideas and experiences.

For some users, the bare quality of typed text allows for a greater flight of imagination and fantasy. Chat room banter can seem quite chaotic, especially when there are many people talking, or you have just entered a room and immediately dive into the ongoing flow of overlapping conversations.

There are no visual cues indicating what pairs or groups of people are huddled together in conversation, so the lines of scrolling dialogue seem disjointed (visual chat environments, where users can move their avatars close to each other, have an advantage in this respect). You have to sit back and follow the flow of the text to decipher the themes of conversation and who is talking with whom.

In almost all types of chat environments, you consciously and unconsciously set up mental filters and points of focus that help you screen out "noise" and zoom in your concentration on particular people or topics of discussion. Often, you become immersed in one or two strings of dialogue and filter out the others. With experience, you develop an eye for efficiently reading TextTalk. Some people may be better at this specific cognitive-perceptual task than others. Let's pop you into an excerpt from an ongoing chat room conversation and see if you can figure out what's happening in this "buzzing confusion."

In part, this is due to the fact that during a post-hoc reading of a log, you read at the pace you usually read any written material - which is QUICKLY, but much too quickly to absorb TextTalk. While online, the lag created by people typing and by thousands of miles of busy internet wires forces the conversation into a slower pace. And so you sit back, read, wait, scan backwards and forwards in the dialogue, and think about what to say next. There's more time for those perceptual/cognitive filters and lens to operate. There's also more time for a psychological/emotional context to evolve in your mind - a context that helps you follow and shape the nuances of meaning that are developing in the TextTalk.

You would think that the lack of ftf cues and the buzzing confusion of TextTalk would result in many misunderstandings. If five different conversations are scrolling before your eyes, it would seem easy to lose track of what was said. Situations involving humor and sarcasm usually were the culprits, because that smile, chuckle, or wry tone of voice were missing. But these misunderstandings were always cleared up quickly. A quick explanation accompanied by a simple smiley :) or winky ;) efficiently resolves the confusion. What's fascinating about TextTalk is that people mostly DO understand what others mean, despite the lack of visual and auditory cues. Of course, some chat users may like to play games with the potential ambiguity of TextTalk.

The excerpt that follows is an interesting example of how the lack of ftf cues can make it difficult to tell whether someone is intending humor or irony, and when they are being honest or sly. The use of the winky ;) and smiley :) are sometimes used to indicate irony or sarcasm, but in this excerpt the situation is perfectly ambiguous. The excerpt also illustrates how people play with the ambiguity of identity in chat environments.

Due to lag in network connections, messages do not appear on your screen at a steady pace, which causes temporal "hiccups" in the pacing of the conversation. People also may be fumbling with their typing, typing a long message, pausing to think... but you can't see that. A conversation may accidentally become crisscrossed until both partners get "in sync." Users skilled in online chat - and who have a talent for writing - will create incomplete sentences or ideas that lead the companion into the next message. To allow the other user to express a complex idea, you may need to sit back into a "listener" mode.

Text communication in a chat room or channel often assumes a staccato style. Most of the time people express what they have to say in a brief sentence or two, or in sentence fragments. This style works well when people are joking around and ribbing each other, often in what turns out to be a playful game of "can you top this."

In these kinds of exchanges, it usually doesn't matter too much if the other users' messages arrive on your screen out of the order in which the users may have intended them, since there is no specific logical sequence that is needed for the ideas. It is more of a group "free for all."

Because none of the visual cues of face-to-face encounters are available, people feel the need to quickly test the waters to determine the qualities of the users around them and whom they want to engage. Questions that would be considered less than tactful in face-to-face encounters are a bit more socially acceptable here. Terse inquiries tossed out to a fellow user, or the entire room, might include "Age?", "M/F?", "Married?"

The terse style of talking in chat environments can result in either superficial chat, or a very honest and "to-the-point" discussion of personal issues. One doesn't have the verbose luxury of gradually leading the conversation to a serious topic, so self-disclosures sometimes are sudden and very revealing. The safe anonymity resulting from the lack of ftf contact - as well as people not knowing who you "really" are - also contributes to this honest and open attitude. When a whole room is focused on discussing a single topic, the conversation often takes the form of group free-association.

Unlike face-to-face discussions, it's not clear who is reacting to whom because there is no eye contact. Any given user may be addressing a comment to one other particular user, or to the whole room. If people don't preface their message with the other user's name, it's not easy to tell who is reacting to whom, or if someone is indeed speaking to the whole group.

Messages also appear on your monitor in an intermixed, slightly non-sequential order, unlike face-face-discussions where people typically respond to the idea that was just previously mentioned. The logical flow and transitions of face-to-face encounters are much less apparent. The net result is a group "free association" where ideas bounce off each other and the "owner" and "recipient" of the ideas become secondary. Quite unlike face-to-face encounters, people can send private messages to another user in the room - a message that no one else in the room can see.

There may be very few or no messages appearing on YOUR screen, but the room may not be quiet at all. There may be numerous private exchanges among the other people. In face-to-face encounters, the equivalent would be a silent room filled with telepaths! If you are engaged in one of those private discussions, as well as conversing with people out loud, you are placed in the peculiar situation of carrying on dual social roles - an intimate you and a public you, simultaneously. Even more complex is when you attempt to conduct two (or more) private conversations, perhaps in addition to public ones.

You may be joking privately with user A, conducting a serious personal discussion with user B, and engaging in simple chit-chat out loud with the rest of the room. This highly complex social maneuver requires a psychological mechanism called "dissociation" - the ability to separate out and direct the components of your mind in more than one direction at the same time (the same mechanism that becomes pathologically exaggerated in multiple personality disorders).

It takes a great deal of online experience, mental concentration, and keyboarding skill (eye/hand coordination) to pull it off. There is no equivalent for this in face-to-face encounters, except perhaps having two or more people on different phone lines. But in that situation, your phone partners know you are dividing your efforts to other people, while the chat room users may have no idea of your social juggling.

Humans are funny. Present them with a limit, and they find ways around it. Give them a seemingly simple and straightforward medium, and they find all sorts of ways to creatively fiddle with it. For example, in TextTalk, all you have are some letters to represent your identity. Because there are no visuals in TextTalk, body language is impossible... Or is it? "Parenthetical action" can convey any almost physical expression, some that even may be impossible in the ftf world. Video and audio streaming will make it much easier for people to chat with voices, and facial expressions, and body language - almost like "really" being there. When that happens, will text-only chat environments die out? Will TextTalk become an amusing bit of history in the fast-paced world of internet technology? Perhaps not. Some people strongly prefer the minimalist style of TextTalk. They enjoy the anonymity, as well as the challenge of creatively expressing themselves given the barest bones possible. They see beauty in the clean, simple, quiet flow of scrolling words. Sights and sounds are but extraneous noise that clogs the pure expression of mind and soul.

In the "real" world of five senses, people freely can experiment with language, voice modulation, dress, hand gestures, facial expressions, body language, even perfume - all as ways to communicate nuances in meaning.

In cyberspace, the sensory options are not nearly as numerous or versatile. But that doesn't mean that subtlety is absent. When immersed in a medium that places some restrictions on paths to communicate, humans get downright clever and creative in overcoming the barriers. In the traditional text-only chat environments, users have developed a wide variety of symbols, phrases, and acronyms - a whole new vernacular - to get their ideas and feelings across to their cyberpeers.

In the newer graphical/auditory chat environments, the addition of even relatively simple sight and sound options has provided considerably more elbow room for subtlety in communication and creative self-expression.

Most chat environments have the option of sending a message to someone that other users cannot see. At the Palace, NO ONE can see it, not even a wizard or a god. This is something that is NOT possible in the real world, which makes it feel very special, even powerful as a unique feature of cyberspace. It's almost as if you are telepathically connecting your mind to the recipient of your whisper.

Whispering "Hi Lucy" is a sign of intimacy, something shared just between friends. It's a bit secretive, as if you don't particularly want anyone else to know that you're saying hello. If the recipient of your whisper is someone you don't know well, they may experience your hello as a bit intrusive on their psychic space, or as an "advance" of some sort - perhaps a gesture of friendship, or a hint at desired intimacy. All of this holds true for any chat environment where private messaging is possible. But at the Palace, there's an added visual dimension.

When you whisper, everyone else's avatar fades into grey while just you and the recipient of your message remain in bold, living color - as if the whole world has dropped away, leaving just the two of you. It's a very powerful visual effect. And at the Palace you also are located within the visual space of a room, which is absent in text-only chat. This can significantly affect how whispering is perceived. For example, there's a subtle difference between whispering to someone from the other side of the room (especially a crowded one), as opposed to being right next to them.

Visual chat is a simple way to describe them, although they have gone by a variety of other names, such as multimedia chat, GMUKS (graphical multi-user konversations), and "habitats," a term coined by Randy Farmer, the first to invent them. They are something of a cross between a MOO and a traditional chat room.

As social environments, they are unique in that they are graphical. Rather than limiting users to text-only communications, as in most chat rooms, multimedia programs add a visual dimension that creates the illusion of movement, space, and physicality. It allows people to express their identity VISUALLY, rather than just through written words. The result is a whole new realm for self-expression and social interaction with subtleties and complexities not seen in text-only chat rooms. One excellent example of a multimedia environment is the client/server program called the "Palace." There are basically two visual components to this environment. The first is the backdrop or "room" in which people interact with each other. There are hundreds of Palace sites located across the internet, many with their own unique graphical themes for the collection of rooms that make up the site.

The oldest and one of the most populated sites is the "Main Mansion" which has consisted of approximately 30 rooms, including a bar, a game room, bedrooms, a study, a beach, a moor, and several surrealistic scenes, such as the orbit of an alien planet and an underground cave that looks like Hades. Users can move freely within and between the rooms. Like characters in comic strips, you communicate with others via typed text that appears in balloons that pop out from your head or body. Head? Body? This is the second visual feature of Palace: "avatars" or "props." Although these words often are used interchangeably, there is a slight distinction in the minds' of some users.

Avatars refer to pictures, drawings, or icons that users choose to represent themselves. Props are objects that users may add to their avatars or place into the Palace room or give to another person. No doubt, the avatar-driven lifestyle at the Palace sets up a self-selection process that determines which users decide to stay, and in some cases almost LIVE there.

People who love graphics - and especially those who love costumes and masks - often make Palace their home away from home. This anonymity is very different than that found in text-only chat environments, where only the name you have chosen publicizes your online identity. At the Palace, you also have a costume. Wearing a costume at a real-life party does indeed filter out many of the physical features of your identity. You are somewhat "anonymous." But the costume also symbolically highlights aspects of who you are. It amplifies one of your interests, some facet of your personality or lifestyle, or something you wish for. As we will see, the same is true of avatars in a multimedia community.

There are two types of Avatars. The first are the standard set of "smileys" that come with the Palace program . Inspired by ASCII smileys, these faces are available to all users. They come in a set that displays basic human emotions and behavioral signals - happy, sad, angry, winking, sleeping/bored, blushing, head-nodding, head-shaking. The user also can change the color of the face or add to it one or more props, such as hats, wigs, scarfs, devil horns, a halo, a glass of beer, a bicycle, etc. Because the faces and props can be mixed and matched, users have at their disposal an almost infinite array of combinations to express themselves. As such, the standard set of avs are designed very cleverly and offer a wide range of behavioral and emotional expression.

On one level, his perception is inaccurate because the standard smileys and props are quite clever and artistic. On another level, though, he quite accurately touches on a pervasive attitude among many Palace members. The standard avs are associated with newbies, whom some consider a lower class in the Palace population. They are fresh arrivals who do not understand the Palace culture and have not yet established their identity and status in it.

In the early days of Palace, new users who had not registered their software (i.e., paid for it) were restricted to using only the standard avs and props. They did not have the power create their OWN customized avatars, which is tantamount to establishing your own unique identity among a horde of avatars.

Even for users who have that power, failing to create and display your own personal avs is taken as a sign that you don't know how to. The bottom line: to wear a standard smiley is to look like a newbie. This leads to the second major category of avatars - those created by the members themselves. This is the key to what is perhaps the most fascinating aspect of the Palace. Visually, you can be anything you want. Only your graphics skills and imagination limit you. Early in the development of Palace, Bumgardner noticed that people highly preferred the custom faces over the more anonymous smileys.

In cyberspace, most people don't want to be totally anonymous. But they DO like control over how their identity is expressed. They like it a lot. Hang out at the Palace for any length of time and a seemingly endless parade of avs of all shapes, colors, and styles pass before your eyes. Visit the Palace everyday, and within a few weeks your prop file can blossom to 10, 20, 30 megs. What kinds of avatars do members create for themselves? Some are pictures or icons borrowed from internet archives, scanned from hardcopy, or taken from other digital sources.

Users might edit or combine these pictures according to their particular tastes. Some artistic members create props from scratch, although this is a fairly rare - and envious - skill. The technical and artistic ability one demonstrates through personal avs is an important source of self-esteem and social status.

Animal avatars are some of the most popular at the Palace. Some people come as their pets. Because animals symbolize certain traits or attributes in myth as well as popular culture (e.g., strength, loyalty, grace, independence, cunning, transcendence), the animal chosen for an avatar probably bears psychological significance to the person - perhaps representing some real aspect of his or her identity, or some characteristic admired by the person.

While younger users (adolescents) may be more inclined to don cartoon costumes, older members frequently use them as well. The psychological significance of the cartoon character probably affects the choice made by the user. People select characters with whom they identify or admire.

Some cartoon characters have very specific cultural significance and may even represent archetypal personality types (e.g., Bugs Bunny as the confident trickster; Aladdin's genie as the powerful but benevolent friend).

Celebrity avatars tend to follow trends in popular culture. And like items in popular culture, they may quickly become epidemic and then disappear. There may be a variety of motives behind the use of these avs. People may use them to express personality traits or social issues that are associated with the celebrity's image (sensuality, intelligence, power, corruption, rebellion, etc.).

The user may identify with, desire, or be poking fun at these attributes. They may hope to bolster their self-esteem and identity by establishing their connection to the celebrity. They may simply wish to display a knowledge of current events in pop culture. Everyone has a dark or "evil" side to his or her personality. The definition of "evil" varies from person to person, although usually it has something to do with malicious, aggressive fantasies and/or feelings of guilt.

While some members may wear an evil av as their facade for the evening (which may reflect their mood at the time), others may "flash" it as a momentary cue to others. Mess with wizards, for example, and they may flash their evil av as a warning that they're getting annoyed and may pin, gag, or kill you. Some people may use evil or aggressive avatars as a way (consciously or unconsciously) to alienate or "put off" other people. This might indicate their anxiety about intimacy and being vulnerable.

Most users do not use pictures of themselves as their primary avatars. People prefer the partial anonymity of expressing only limited aspects of their personality through imaginative props. Or they simply enjoy the creative fun of experimenting with new identities through their avs.

In more rare cases, members find the use of real face avs to be an uncomfortable, dissociative experience. "I have a picture of myself in the prop file but I really don't like to use it any longer than it takes for me to show it to a new friend," said River, a wizard. "It is a little disturbing to sit here at home and see myself speaking in cartoon balloons in a non-reality. Whew!!!!" When users do present pictures of their real faces, it may be a gesture of honesty and/or intimacy - a sign of friendship, or even romance. Showing one's real face av can be a very poignant experience.

Several members have described to me encounters when an intimate conversation culminated in their companion showing a picture of themselves. "That moment will stay with me for a long time to come," one member stated, "The value I placed on that particular moment was, friendship, trust, a sense of oneness." This same member described how there seems to be a pattern when an entire group feels compelled to use their real faces - what he called "face nite."

For that period of time, the intimacy and friendship level reaches a point where people wish to step out of their masks and out of their anonymity. They want be as "real" as possible. Some members develop an entire set of real face avatars. Idiosyncratic Avatars become strongly associated with a specific member - almost as if it is that person's trademark. In some cases the avatar may be highly unusual or creative. Sometimes it is quite simple. Yet its association to the particular user is so strong that others experience it uniquely as that person. While trading props is a common practice, the owner of an idiosyncratic av rarely gives it away. It would be like giving one's identity to someone else to use.

Conscientious members also don't "steal"an idiosyncratic av and use it as their own. They respect its integrity. If someone does steal and attempts to wear an idio av, they must be willing to put up with criticism by the friends of the owner. Positional Avatars are designed by the member to be placed into specific positions within the Palace rooms. The avatar may be created for a certain type of environment, or may be designed specifically for a single room or even a very specific spot within a room.

These avatars illustrate how the graphics of the Palace rooms are NOT simply "background" that have little impact on behavior. Some members are exquisitely sensitive to the graphical environment. Creating props to match and interact with the features of the room is a highly creative activity. Such avatars also are a sign of status. By displaying them, the member is demonstrating a sophisticated awareness of the Palace environment as well as technical know-how in prop editing.

Many, if not all, people have conscious or unconscious fantasies of omnipotence. These types of avs seem to be most common among male adolescent users. In some cases the power theme is benign. Sometimes not, which may be a variation of the "evil" avatar. Because competition invariably accompanies displays of power, members seem to vie with each other in creating the most "awesome" power av. This competition is probably more common among the adolescent users. Members who persistantly display power avs may be troubled by underlying feelings of helplessness and insecurity.

Offenders first are warned by wizards, prop-gagged (forced into the standard smiley), and, if necessary, disconnected from the server. Adapting to these house rules, some users create avatars of partially naked or scantily clothed figures. Mischievious members sometimes push the envelope by wearing avs that test the limits and ambiguities of the rules.

Supreme court justices have had a hard time defining what is pornographic, so the task has been no easier for the officials who run the EC sites. Even though the rules have become very specific about what body parts can and cannot be visible in an av, borderline cases always pop up. Female seductive avatars tend to be more common than male - although these female avs sometimes are "manned" by male users.

In fact, the general impression among members is that males are more likely to prop up as females, especially seductive females, than women dressing up as males. Members usually wear seductive avs to draw attention to themselves. This works very well. Male users, especially guests, quickly flock to a sexy female form. The owner may be interested in harmless flirting, or (less frequently) be advertising his or her availability for cybersex. Some people wearing seductive avs wish to be admired as an attractive, sexy individual, without necessarily being interested in flirting or cybersex. "I have some very sexy stuff given to me by friends (all men!)," said one female member. The competition in creating and displaying props is especially visible for seductive avatars. "It's interesting how some of the women at the Palace are getting into more and more elaborate sexy props.

Almost as if it's a contest," noted one member. "But then, some of the guys too are into 'comparing' props!" For men, the competition usually involves power props, rather than seductive ones. As one member stated, "the stag with the biggest rack thing, ey?" A seductive, sexy, or simply "attractive" avatar can have a powerful impact on other members. One member described how his prop of a cartoon animal didn't seem to be getting him much attention from females. Most of them wouldn't talk to him. Curious about whether he could alter this situation, he searched the net and found a picture of Brad Pitt which he turned into a prop.

If he happened to be wearing his cartoon prop and found that he was being ignored by a woman, he would move to another room, switch to Brad Pitt, and then return. Or he would switch to Pitt right in front of her. Nine times out of ten, he said, the woman would strike up a conversation with him even if he hadn't said a word. He even established a relationship with someone who eventually wanted to meet him face-to-face. "The pic got her attention," he concluded, "but in the end it was me that won her over."

The curious thing about this phenomenon is that members KNOW that people are not their avatars. Just because a prop is pretty to look at doesn't mean that the user is. Nevertheless, that seductive av has tremendous drawing power. Perhaps some people enjoy the illusion of interacting with (and hopefully winning over) an attractive person.

Perhaps, as many critics of contemporary culture claim, some people can't resist the temptation of superficial appearances, despite knowing better. Or perhaps some people are just curious, "Who *IS* that person using that sexy av?" Other members may display seductive avs simply to be admired for their skill in knowing how to create a seductive av.

Because the Palace often feels like an ongoing party where people are going to flirt, playfully compete, vie for attention, and strut their stuff, it is almost a prerequisite that every experienced member owns a seductive av of some type. "Getting away with something" is an intrinsic component of the Palace culture, as Bumgardner intended. Having at least one seductive av is a cultural must. Of course, there are exceptions to every rule. There is such a wide variety of avatars that it's impossible to neatly classify them all. The same is true of personality styles (which is the origin of the prop).

Odd/shocking avatars are unusual, strange, and sometimes downright bizarre pictures - perhaps revealing people who like to surprise, goof on, or even startle and outrage others. Truly bizarre pictures might make you wonder about the person's grasp of social appropriateness, or even their mental health. Such very unusual avs are most popular among adolescents - for whom extreme behavior is a way to express independence and individuality, and to test the limits.

Abstract avatars may be used by people who enjoy enjoy symmetry, are good (non-verbal) conceptual thinkers, and/or are inclined towards visual artistic endeavors.

Billboard avatars are announcements of some sort - political, philosophical, personal. They are used by those who have something to say and are not reluctant to display their thoughts in a commercialized type format.

Lifestyle avatars, which are quite common and varied, depict some significant aspect of a person's life - usually something to do with occupation, hobby, or personal habit. It may be a way to attract like-minded individuals.

Matching avatars are designed to accompany each other and indicate the connection or bonding between the pair of members. Considerable imaginative and technical skills may go into creating such avatars.

Clan avatars are worn by members of the same social group, some might even say "gang." These avs tend to be similar in basic design with slight variations to differentiate each one from the others. As such, each user announces his/her allegiance to the clan by adopting its collective visual appearance, while also maintaining some measure of individuality. It reminds me of the songs in some bird species.

The species identifies itself and its members by a basic template that serves as the collective song. Yet each individual bird adds a small unique variation to that template in order to signify its individuality. Clan avs are found almost exclusively among adolescents for whom belonging to a peer group - and conforming to its standards - is a developmental hallmark.

Animated avatars contain motion, such as an eye tearing, a bird flying, or a flag waving. By visually diplaying "behavior" they can express a wide and subtle range of psychological meaning. Tapping a finger, blinking one's eyes, banging one's head against the wall - there are infinite expressive possibilties. The motion usually is cyclical and repetitious, which - depending on the type of avatar - may convey a feeling of persistance, determination, mindlessness, or rhythmic peacefulness.

The default size for an avatar is about 40x40 pixels. That's about as big as your average computer icon. When members create their first avatar, it's usually this size. They're pretty happy with their accomplishment, until they realize that other people have much BIGGER props. It takes a bit more know-how to master the technique of building large avs.

Some members quickly get into a competitive feeling about whose is biggest - although the contest quickly ends at about 130x130 pixels, which is the technical limit. People may rely on prop size to gain attention and admiration. I've heard some members state that younger users, especially male adolescents, like large props, while women tend to wear smaller props in general than men. These hypotheses certainly are amenable to quantitative research. The general consensus among Palatians is that "bigger is not better." Big avs sometimes are considered impolite.

They take up a lot of precious space in a crowded room. They're a bit ostentatious. What matters more than size is the quality and style of your avatar. What matters is how you apply it to express yourself. "It's not the size of the prop, but how you use it." Like masks of any kind, avatars hide and reveal at the same time. Behind it, people can conceal some personal things about themselves, but the av also selectively amplifies other aspects of their personalities. It may reveal something about the member that otherwise is not immediately obvious - maybe not even obvious if you met that person in real life. Maybe not even obvious to the owners themselves. What users express in their props is not always a conscious choice. Sometimes it's unconscious.

Psychoanalysts would describe them as the constellation of "introjects," "internalizations," and "identifications" that comprises our intrapsychic world. On a daily basis, we juggle and shift between several rather distinct selves, sometimes without being fully aware that we are doing it. How, when, and why these different facets of our identity manifest themselves is the story of our lives.

In the multimedia communities of cyberspace, you can tell a lot about people by examining their collection of avatars and how they use them. Each avatar reflects a distinct aspect of the individual's personality and lifestyle - whether it is a mood, an interest pattern, a social role, one's attitudes and values, or a wished-for state of being.

Many people have persona that are seductive, powerful, formal/sophisticated, silly/playful, and artistic/poetic. These may represent universal or archetypal sectors of personality. Most people cherish at least one original avatar because it represents their birth identity in the Palace community. It's like an old, reliable friend. Almost everyone has a primary, all-purpose av that they use most of the time. It's the familiar home base, the image they feel most identified with and most comfortable wearing.

Active members are always creating new avs. One's collection is a balance of new and old persona, which reflects the balance between experimenting with new identities and holding onto the familiar, stable aspects of self. The size and variations in one's collection probably reflects the extent to which the person explores and experiments with personal identity.

Many people have a secret avatar that they use when they don't want others to know who they are, as well as an avatar they wear when they're with friends - an appearance that readily identifies them to their friends, often that birth or primary avatar. Curiously, many people have an av which they really like, but aren't sure why they like it. It is a conscious reminder of an unconscious aspect of identity.

On the simplest level, they act as conversation pieces. If you can think of nothing else to say, express an interest in someone's prop. Talking about props is one of the most common topics of discussion at the Palace. It greases the social interaction, especially with people whom you are meeting for the first time. It's like discussing the weather - except people are more personally invested in their props than they are in whether it's rainy or sunny. On a more complex level, changes in avatars convey changes in mood and intention, without the person necessarily having to speak.

Many members have told me that what they are wearing affects how they behave, as well as influences how others will react to them. Wear a female seductive prop, or even just a pleasant looking female prop, and you will draw attention, whether you want it or not. If you're annoyed with someone and want to drive them away, put on that skull prop.

Using the brush for painting on the background room image, some users adorn the walls with graffiti, obscene drawings or words. Other mischievous members smear black over an entire room, or they fill the entire room with props, leaving newbies totally confused as to where they are or what's happening. Freud would want to label them "anal expulsive personalities." By "spoofing" someone with the "msay" command, you can throw your voice to make the cartoon text balloon pop out of someone else's head. Or you can make the words hang in mid-air with no body attached. Sometimes, it's hard even for sympathetic people to resist the antics and game-playing.

Users who make rapid, multiple changes of their avatars - especially large avatars - may flood the server, resulting in lag that makes it difficult for people to talk. Usually the person is not aware that he is causing a problem. But sometimes people do it on purpose. It may be a hostile attempt to gain attention, or a jealous ploy to disrupt the socializing in the room. Wizards will warn, pin, or, if necessary, kill for this offense.

Members consider it a social faux pas to place your avatar on top of or too close to another person's prop. Unless the person is a friend who's in the mood to be close, it's an invasion of personal space. "Please get off me!" and You're sitting on me!" are two common complaints. Again, some naive users do this without knowing it is inappropriate, or the person may be lagging and unable to move. But some hostile people deliberately accost others by blocking them. Wizards will warn, pin, or, if necessary, kill for this offense.

Sleepers usually are users who have walked away from their computer. They are completely unresponsive when you talk to them. The social norm is to put up a "BRB" (be right back) sign to indicate your unavailability. Sleepers fail to do this. Although sleepers may be found in text-only chat environments, the experience of them is a bit different in multimedia chat. It feels much more eerie to SEE a person (avatar) in front of you, yet the person fails to react.

By reducing their avatars to a single pixel and their usernames to only one character, members may try to become "invisible" and secretly listen in on conversations. As a type of "lurker," they are acting on voyeuristic tendencies to avoid intimacy and gain a sense of advantage and power over others.

People enjoy so much the ability to express themselves visually through their avatars that it seems self-defeating to avoid this opportunity by hiding. Maybe that says something about eavesdropping.

There are very specific rules about what avatars are acceptable and what ones are not. Unacceptable avs fall into four general categories: overly sexual; overly violent and aggressive; hate avatars (evidence of prejudice concerning gender, homosexuality, religion, ethnicity, and nationality); avatars that promote illegal activities.

Although nudity in avatars is not permitted at the Palace, some people nevertheless flash their naughty pictures. They may be goofing around with their friends, advertising their availability for cybersex, attempting to shock other people (like the typical exhibitionist), or defiantly and perhaps masochistically begging to be killed by a wizard.

In private rooms, behind locked doors, people engaged in cybersex will display pornographic props to one another. Because this is not public behavior, it is not punished. The exhibitionist and rebellious psychology of the prop-dropper is probably similar to the flasher, with the exception that they attempt to dissociate themselves from their "dropping." In the mind of a Freudian, the scatological implications of this behavior are very signficant. Stealing someone's avatar and wearing it is a no-no. Stealing someone's avatar, wearing it, and also using that person's name (or a variation of it) is a real no-no. You are abducting their entire identity. Palace users are not limited to the standard background graphics. The creators of Palace intentionally designed it as a virtual world where users could express themselves by shaping the environment. At the Member's Only Palace site, people could create their own room using any background image of their choice.

Cooperative "set-dressing" in these rooms developed into a complex art form. These custom rooms became the focal points of friendship subgrouping and cliques. If you are ambitious, you can create your own Palace site on your own server, which gives you total control over the look of all the rooms.

Each new space -whether it is a single customized room or a whole new site - will reflect the personality of its creator and will draw people of similar temperament. In order to attract people to a site, attempts are made to make the new environments as psychologically appealing to as many users as possible. Some multimedia worlds are 3D. Usually the view also is first person, so you live "inside" your avatar, looking out into the world much as you do in real life, without seeing your own avatar (body). You have to move through the graphical space in order to see other avatars and objects that may be hidden from view.

3D advocates like the feeling of "immersion" that such worlds create. You feel like you are really there, in the environment. Some advocates claim that this 3D living creates heightened emotional reactions because it mimics the sensory experience of the real world. Things come towards you, or withdraw. You don't know what's around the next corner. There is an element not only of realism, but even suspense. The problem with a 3D graphical experience is that it requires a lot of computing power and speed that cannot (yet) be handled too well by internet band width.

The result may be a slow, jerky experience that feels disjointed, unreal, and that jars the brain. Even under ideal conditions, some people don't feel comfortable with the "head in a box" or "tunnel vision" view of 3D, first-person worlds. Lacking peripheral vision, some people feel closed in, claustrophobic. The Palace is a 2D, third person experience. You look down onto the scene that includes your avatar and everyone else's avatar. Some people like this transcendent and somewhat paradoxical experience of being above but also in the scene. You get to see yourself, the way other people do.

You move yourself about in the environment and then sit back to see what happens. Your perspective of the scene and what people are saying may seem more "objective." You may feel more free. There may even be a magical, mystical sensation to witnessing oneself within the world.

Many mystical traditions emphasize the transcendent awareness that is the "observing self." The 2D worlds may address an archetypic need for such transcendence. This observing awareness is paradoxical. It simultaneously exists within the world and transcends it - a paradox that is manifested in the 2D virtual setting. Some Palace members take delight in the objective/

subjective fluidity of being in the scene and above it, at the same time. The avatar appears as an independent entity that actually is a manifestation of your personality and will. Separate but connected. It can be like an artistic creation, a self portrait. It's an "out there" expression of what's inside. It's possible that when first person, 3D worlds becomes more sophisticated with the advance of technology, people will prefer them. On the other hand, some people may always favor third person, 2D environments. These differences in preference may reflect differences in cognitive and personality style.

Avatar psychotherapy

In cyberspace, the term "avatar" is used to describe one's personal manifestation in a virtual world. It may be the visual image you create for yourself, as well as the psychological character or persona you present to others. The term comes from the Hindu religion in which it refers to the various forms that gods chose to manifest themselves in the human realm. Using computer-generated virtual environments, "avatar psychotherapy" could be the exploration of the client's healthy and problematic identities by exploring the manifestation of those identities within imaginary scenarios.

Using psychoanalytic terms, we would say that the client teases out, amplifies, explores, and therapeutically develops the various "representations," "identifications," and "internalizations" that make up their intrapsychic world, that are the nuts and bolts of their overall sense of self. The techniques of avatar psychotherapy could draw on a variety of psychotherapeutic approaches:

- — exploring childhood memories in order to shape a more healthy life narrative
- — the interpretation, reworking, and mastery of dreams, daydreams, and fantasy by reenacting them
- — realistic and imaginary role playing of current life situations involving family, friends, and peers, including the reversal of roles
- — creating dramatic "plays" to explore clients' identities as reflected in the mythology of their favorite literature and movies
- — working with transference and countertransference reactions via imaginary scenarios
- — developing and "installing" new, more adaptive facets of self

Therapists can participate in, direct, or simply observe these virtual enactments. When they participate, the may work with transference/countertransference dynamics as manifested in the avatars they chose or that are chosen for them by their clients. It's even possible that the client and therapist could create automated software characters to participate in the scenes. The basic assumption of avatar psychotherapy is that all of the personae created in the virtual scenario are the various manifestations of the client's psyche.

Those avatars concretize the complex constellations of memories, fears, wishes, idealizations, and expectations that comprise the client's sense of self. Those avatars give clients the opportunity to amplify, explore, modify, and develop those sectors of self. However, giving life to those avatars is not the ultimate goal of the therapy. Immersion in the virtual field could become a game with no conclusion, a distraction from or even an active avoidance of the final goal that is assimilation of the personae into a unified, cohesive self where the various facets of self are joined together seamlessly. The ultimate goal is carrying the newly integrated self forward from the virtual world into the in-person world.

Identity Management

The "asynchronous" communication of e-mail allows members to participate in the ongoing virtual meeting at their own convenience and at their own pace. Some of the unique features of asynchronous, typed-text communication also may alter the interpersonal dynamics of the group, which offers the opportunity to better understand and improve how the group functions. A group as well may use "message board" formats to meet online. When creating an e-mail list, obviously it's important to make sure that everyone has an e-mail account. Extending the group into cyberspace when some people don't use e-mail is a bad idea. It will encourage subgrouping, miscommunication, and perhaps conflict.

Doing so may even be a symptom of preexisting conflict and an acting out of hostility against subgroups or individual scapegoats. It's equally important to assess how much people know about using e-mail in general and an e-mail list in particular. Some study says that they use e-mail "a lot" (since it's fashionable) when in reality they may only be casual users who barely understand the basics. As a result, setting up the list may be a slow, sometimes frustrating process.

On the positive side, that process can serve as an opportunity for people to familiarize themselves with e-mail lists before the actual online meeting begins. It's a good idea to have a facilitator or "host" for the list - someone who can set up the list and has some technical understanding of how lists work, as well as some experience in the customs and social dynamics of a list.

E-mail can be a fascinating, subtle tool for communicating - different, in many respects, from talking. Some even consider it an art form. It might be a good idea to recommend some reading about e-mail to the group.

There are many practical uses for the list. On the most basic level, it can be used for announcements, scheduling in-person meetings, and generally serve as a substitute for hardcopy memos. However, limiting the list to this function alone - a kind of "memo mentality" - falls short of utilizing its full potential.

Memo mentality ignores how the list can be a group MEETING with many other possible applications. It can be used in a collaborative effort to edit, revise, and approve a document. The group can prepare for and afterwards discuss an in-person meeting. Under ideal conditions, the list can be an effective alternative for in-person meetings by encouraging open discussions of issues and decision-making.

Extending the group into cyberspace can have a double-edged effect. On the one hand, the exchange of messages via the list may draw out or highlight the preexisting interpersonal dynamics of the group.

Typed text has a way of making things stand out in bold relief, sometimes "demonstrating the obvious" in a very eye-catching, rubbing-one's-nose-in-it fashion. On the other hand, an online meeting also may alter the dynamics of the group because it entails a change in the boundaries of time, place, and communication style. For example:

— *Pacing*: Because e-mail involves asynchronous communication, people can speak to the group whenever they want and as frequently as they want. Avid e-mail users may have more input into the discussion than casual or inexperienced users, possibly altering in a dramatic way the usual in-person pattern of participation.

— *Writing, not talking*: Typed-text usually forces people to be more concise and to-the-point, resulting in a filtering out of extraneous conversation that typically pads a face-to-face meeting. The e-mail discussion may feel more efficient to some people, or blunt to others. Some members may be frustrated by the tedium of having to type everything they want to say, feeling a f2f dialogue is easier and more thorough. Because e-mail involves writing and not speaking, those with superior writing skills will have a communicative advantage. They may not be the same people who have the verbal advantage in an in-person meeting. Those who are ignored, interrupted, or talked-over during a f2f meeting may have a stronger voice in cyberspace. Those who dominate an in-person meeting may lose some of their influence online.

— *Disinhibition:* People can' t see you or hear your voice in an e-mail discussion, which results in a "masking" effect and psychological disinhibition. People may be more willing to express thoughts and feelings that they otherwise would keep to themselves during an in-person meeting. As a result, new ideas may pop up. Surprising opinions are expressed. Conflicts that were previously warded off now rise to the surface. In an ideal situation, this disinhibiting effect can jostle a group into new and productive lines of discussion. In unfortunate circumstances, the uncovering of hidden problems may destabilize the group, reducing it's ability to communicate and work effectively. In-person meetings will be needed to remedy that situation.

— *Permanent Record:* Any member easily can save all the group's message to an archive. Everything that was said online can be preserved indefinitely. This permanent record can come in handy in reviewing who said what and when, how decisions were made, and for attaining a bird' s eye view of the course of a discussion. Without visual and verbal cues, it's sometimes easy to misread the meaning or emotion within someone's message - particularly if you happen to be having a bad day. Going back to read a message at a later date can help you see it in a fresh light, with a new mental set and a bit more objectivity.

Because e-mail meetings are very different than being in-person, some people may show resistance to participating. That resistance may manifest itself in several ways: infrequent messages sent to the list; brief or unsubstantial discussions; frequent pleas for in-person meetings; habitual private (backchannel) e-mail or private in-person discussions (rather than bringing issues to the list); critical comments about using a list; and other assorted direct and indirect expressions of hostility.

In rare circumstances some people may staunchly refuse to participate, which can create considerable uneasiness and distrust in the group. There are a variety of possible reasons for resistance:

- Being unfamiliar or uncomfortable with using computers, e-mail, or e-mail lists. Some people may need time and experience to adapt; a little bit of training could be helpful.
- A fear of displaying one's writing abilities. It's very helpful to establish a norm where all writing styles are accepted - including being casual and making errors in spelling and grammar.
- A fear of "going public." People may worry that someone might save their messages and later use them as "ammunition" against them. This anxiety may coincide with the worry that people outside the group may have access to the list or may be given e-mail by a group member. Such concerns may be a low-level symptom of preexisting distrust within the group. From the get-go, emphasizing the importance of list confidentiality can help alleviate some of these worries.
- Angry withdrawal, indifference. These barriers are most likely a symptom of preexisting interpersonal dynamics within the group. The disinhibiting effect of e-mail communication may help people discuss and resolve these issues, but don't count on it.

In particular, the disinhibiting effect of e-mail could lead people to state things that they refrain from bringing to the in-person meeting. Sometimes the list discussions may even evolve into a kind of "subconscious" voicing of issues that are actively avoided in-person. It is possible to work through these issues on the list, allowing the beneficial effects to seep into the f2f meetings without openly discussing them in those meetings. However, the best approach is to head off the dissociation before it becomes too deeply embedded.

Under ideal conditions, in-person and e-mail discussions will complement and enrich each other. The group will come to recognize the pros and cons of each realm. It will learn to maximize the advantages and minimize the disadvantages of each. The degree of success is the degree to which the group can effectively integrate the two.

When the group moves fluidly from one realm to the other, when both realms give expression to all important group functions - brainstorming, decision-making, problem-solving, socializing, conflict resolution - then the group has fully succeeded in extending itself into cyberspace.

The username you choose, the details you do or don't indicate about yourself, the information presented on your personal web page, the persona or avatar you assume in an online community - all are important aspects of how people manage their identity in cyberspace. Identity is a very complex aspect of human nature. Here are five interlocking factors that are useful in navigating that maze of how people manage who they are in cyberspace:

Cyberspace offers a niche for each of these specific facets of selfhood. Some people even talk about how we can "deconstruct" ourselves online. Online communication tools even give you the choice about whether you want people to see how you look or hear your voice. The desire to remain anonymous reflects the need to eliminate those critical features of your identity that you do NOT want to display in that particular environment or group. The desire to lurk - to hide completely - indicates the person's need to split off his entire personal identity from his observing of those around him: he wants to look, but not be seen. Compartmentalizing or dissociating one's various online identities like this can be an efficient, focused way to manage the multiplicities of selfhood.

Cyberspace living is yet another manifestation of this shifting, juggling maneuver. It gives people the opportunity to focus on and develop a particular aspect of who they are. It may even give people the chance to express and explore facets of their identity that they do not express in their face-to-face world. Everyone in Jim's in-person world may not know that he is a romantic medieval knight in an online role-playing game. However, the importance of integrating the assorted components of selfhood should not be ignored.

Most of the time we will criticize a person's need to hurt other people and applaud compassion. But it's not necessary to present universal truisms about good and bad. Subjectively, a person can feel shame, guilt, fear, anxiety, or hatred about some aspect of their identity, while accepting and appreciating other aspects. People also strive to attain new, idealized ways of being. Those who act out in cyberspace - who are in some way hurting or violating the rights of others, or hurting themselves - are usually discharging some negatively charged aspect of their psyche. This purely cathartic act often goes no where. An insecure, passive-aggressive person gets stuck in an endless stream of online arguments. Others may use cyberspace as a opportunity to exercise their positive characteristics, or to develop new ones in a process of "self-actualization."

Online romances, even those involving a clearly recognized element of fantasy, can be growth-promoting. In some cases people may express a negative trait in an attempt to work through it. They are trying to transform the negative feature of their identity into a positive one, or perhaps change their attitude about that feature. A gay person who learns to accept his homosexuality as a result of participation in an online support group has changed the valence from negative to positive.

The various environments and styles of communication on the internet serve as a flexible testing ground for exploring those intertwining pluses and minuses. In back-channel e-mail, a fellow lurker in a listserv for professionals may help the quiet person learn the value of being silent in some situations. In a chat room, that same quiet person comes to realize the freedom and delight of spontaneously opening up, and how that leads to friendships.

In some online groups - for example, professional e-mail lists - you are expected to present yourself as you truly are. You don't pretend to be someone other than your true identity. Other groups in cyberspace encourage or even require that you assume an imaginary persona, as in the fantasy worlds of MOOs, MUDs, and other game environments. In multimedia chat communities, you have no choice but to wear an imaginative looking avatar to represent yourself.

Many other environments fall somewhere in between reality and fantasy. You could get away with pretending to be someone very different than who you are, or you could alter just a few features - like your name, occupation, or physical appearance - while retaining your other true characteristics. No one will know, especially in text-only environments. In fact, you don't know for sure if other people are altering their identities, or how many people are altering their identities. This power to alter oneself often interlocks with dissociation and valence. Hidden positive and negative parts of oneself may seek expression in an imaginary identity that comes to life online.

Similarly, in cyberspace, people choose a specific communication channel to express themselves. There are a variety of possibilities and combinations of possibilities, each choice giving rise to specific attributes of identity. People who rely on text communication prefer the semantics of language and perhaps also the linear, composed, rational, analytic dimensions of self that surface via written discourse. They may be the "verbalizers" that have been described in the cognitive psychology literature - as opposed to "visualizers" who may enjoy the more symbolic, imagistic, and holistic reasoning that is expressed via the creation of avatars and web graphics. Some people prefer synchronous communication - like chat - which reflects the spontaneous, free-form, witty, and temporally "present" self. Others are drawn to the more thoughtful, reflective, and measured style of asynchronous communication, as in message boards and e-mail.

There are personalities that want to show and not receive too much by using web cams or creating web pages; to receive and not show too much by lurking or web browsing; and still others who want to dive into highly interactive social environments where both showing and receiving thrive. The media chosen can intimately interlock with the degree of identity integration and dissociation, and with the extent to which a person presents a real or imaginary self.

7

Counselling: Theory and Practice

Every living being in existence, be it a plant, an animal or a human being, is born with a potential, and has the longing, the urge, the drive to fulfill its potential, to live itself. The longing and the urge of every living being is, to discover these intrinsic qualities that want to be lived and shared in existence. The plant kingdom and the animal kingdom are living their essence already. The program is inbuilt. A dog is born a dog, lives as a dog, and dies as a dog. He is spontaneous in that expression of life. He does not think whether he should be anything else than a dog. The same is happening with a rose, or a lotus or any other kind of flower or plant. It grows and becomes that which it is meant to become. And in that growing it continues to live in oneness. No animal or plant ever experiences separation. The human being seems to be different. The human being is born with a potential, and then it is up to him or her to nourish that potential, to develop it, to realize the essence, or to forget it. The whole focus aligns itself with the demands of surroundings. Very seldom somebody tells us: "Be!" Through the conditioning of becoming suffer many experiences of separation, and alienate ourselves more and more from who are already. This alienation is the main cause of suffering in the world. Counselling can initiate a healing process for this suffering.

What it call healing in this time is not just healing of the physical body, it is also healing of many misunderstandings of the mind, of the past, that has created wounds. These wounds are carried in the aura, the energy field surrounding and pervading each person. These wounds can have their origin in this life, or in past lives. It seems that suffering pattern repeat themselves. A family, the suffering pattern gets inherited, gets transferred from grandparents to parents to children to grand children and so on. The habits, the behavior patterns, difficulties in life, the mindsets seem to be very similar. This is what could call Karma. Underneath that conditioning is waiting to be discovered the true nature of each human being.

Counselling is using the psychological insights of this time to help the client to move from the personality to the individuality. It is using the expressions of this body—mind to move beyond the body—mind. It is using language, communication, emotions, sentiments, physical sensations, sensory experiences, be they visual, auditory, kinesthetic, olfactory or gustatory, as a key to unlock the door of the inner treasures. A great discovery is possible to find what is actually behind all these sensory experiences. As the counsellor is in contact with his/her own potential, he/she creates an energy field in which the client can resonate and uncover his/her own potential. From that essence the client can discover the very specific elements and traits of their individuality. He/she can discover the flower that is there already, the flower that he/she is meant to be in this life. The client can understand and stop trying to be someone else. Just like a rose does not try to become a lotus, but enjoys being a rose, the client can uncover and rejoice in what he/she is already. As the essence is not in any way affected by personality and by the change of personality, counselling can help the client to accept, embrace, enjoy anything that this lifestream in this body-mind is expressing.

Most of the suffering in life happens, because feel split, separate and disconnected from source. Suffering happened because it feel pushed or pulled, feel under pressure of some outside forces, where it become slaves and victims of outer circumstances, rather than masters. This victimization and suffering is a misunderstanding. It is due to energy moving out trying to identify with objects outside.

Counselling helps the client to turn the energy around and discover who is there already. The strange phenomenon is, that whatever is being experienced in the moment, be it sadness, anger, desperateness, hopelessness or joy, happiness and love, all become a door to discover ones individuality. As any emotion or state is experienced totally without rejection, without trying to make it different, without hope of any change, the very experience becomes pleasant. In the willingness to fully experience that which is in this moment, the negative or painful happening transforms into joy. Now why is that? It is because the pain of any negative experience lies in the interpretation that things should be different.

The moment one becomes one with the experience, the byproduct is joy, love, relaxation into who one is. The astonishing phenomenon is that in becoming one with any emotion, sentiment, or experience, the negative aspect simply disappears. The mysterious discovery is, that anything that was always desired outside, like happiness, bliss, peace, love and freedom, can be rediscovered as being already present inside. Everything that a human being is looking for, is running after, like running after money, a bigger house, a bigger car, a more interesting love partner, is basically an attempt to fulfill this need for happiness, bliss, peace, love and freedom. Every desire tries to fulfill a basic need of returning back to oneness. But once, willing to turn in and look what is there, never moved from this oneness. In that recognition a relaxation can happen, and the energy that is represented in the color and may have been rejected, can be welcomed home. In that very welcome, a healing happens, because oneness happens. The byproduct of that oneness is joy, love and bliss and peace.

In counselling, when a facilitator supports the client to simply see and recognize what is, without any hope of being different, the same phenomenon of becoming one is evoked. As the counsellor supports the client to fully experience what is, the energy that was trapped in fighting what is, becomes available. Since everything that fighting in ourselves is also reflected in the outer world, fight the same things outside of ourselves also. The moment, stop fighting ourselves and experience that which is in its totality, discover the love and acceptance inside. The whole gestalt changes, the whole way of seeing the world changes.

While schools of therapy have argued that different theories produce differing and nonequivalent outcomes, this position has been challenged on numerous occasions. Fiedler first observed that therapists of differing orientations were very similar in their views of the "ideal therapy." Sundland and Barker reported that more experienced therapists tended to be more similar, regardless of their theoretical orientation. In their extensive review of the subject, Gelso and Carter stated that "most clients will profit about equally from the different therapies". They go on to suggest that the effect of process and relationship do differ among therapies and that some clients may do better with one approach than with another, based upon these two factors. Stiles, Shapiro and Elliott argued that

a) common features shared by all psychotherapies underlie or override differences in therapists' verbal techniques and
b) these common features are responsible for the general equivalence in effectiveness.

Process and relationship, then, may be as relevant as theoretical conceptualization of the problem. How do counselors choose a particular counseling theory? Among the alternatives are:

a) the orientation of one's initial training program;
b) one's own philosophy or life view; and/or
c) one's therapeutic experience and evolving therapeutic patterns.

Counselors use theory to explain or conceptualize client problems. In addition, they may use theory to dictate what they do in the counseling process. Theory, whether in pure form or adapted by the individual counselor, can be used to define the nature of the relationship between the counselor and client, to conceptualize the nature of the presenting problem(s), and to define the resulting counseling goals or desired outcomes. While some counselors would also say that theory dictates the types of interventions used in counseling, increasingly the argument is being made that interventions are related more to goals and outcomes than to theoretical conceptualization.

If one examines theoretical integrity today, based upon what counselors faithful to that theory do with clients, a convergence of theories appears to be occurring. Humanistic theories have been infiltrated by some classical behavioral interventions. Behavioral approaches acknowledge the legitimacy of feelings and the appropriateness of affect change.

Cognitive approaches are frequently referred to as "cognitive- behavioral." Systemic approaches utilize many interventions that one can only describe as cognitive in nature. Thus, distinctions between theories are not as clearly defined as one might think, and intervention selection may be only indirectly related, and certainly not dictated by theoretical orientation.

How does the counselor who is working within a consistent theory, be it a textbook theory or a personal theory, choose the interventions to use with a particular client? Logic would hold that the counselor's choice of therapeutic interventions would derive from the conceptualization of the problem(s), thus from the counselor's theory. But the theoretical world of counseling and change isn't quite that neat. From an integrative perspective, that choice is made by relating the intervention directly to the nature or character of the problem being addressed. On the other hand, most client problems are typically multi-dimensional. A problem with negative self-talk ("I'm constantly telling myself I'm no good") is not only cognitive, but would also reflect an affective dimension ("I feel lousy about myself"), a behavioral dimension ("I choose to stay home and watch a lot of TV"), and a systemic dimension ("When I do go out, I avoid contact with others because they find me strange, or I behave strangely and others react to me accordingly").

Even though most problems are multi-dimensional, intervention at any of those dimensions affects the other dimensions, i.e., systemic change may influence affective and/or behavioral dimensions. How, then, does one plan a strategy for counseling interventions if multiple choices exist and "all roads lead to Rome?" A general guideline is that clients are most receptive when the choice of strategy matches their experiencing of the problem. If one examines the variety of counseling interventions that have been described in the professional literature, they tend to fall into four broad categories:

— interventions that produce affective change;

— interventions that produce cognitive change;

— interventions that produce behavioral change; and

— interventions that produce social system change.

In addition, within each of these four categories, one can further differentiate among theories in terms of the counselor skill required to implement the intervention and the level of change produced by the intervention.

Affective interventions: The primary goals of affective interventions are:

(a) to help clients express feelings or feeling states;

(b) to identify or discriminate between feelings or feeling states; or

(c) to alter or accept feelings or feeling states.

Some clients have never learned to identify and/or express their feelings. At a somewhat more complicated level, some clients come to counseling flooded with emotional reactions, overloaded by their awareness of and sensitivity to feelings. Their protective response may be to tune out the emotions, to be confused or disoriented. Interventions that may be used to unblock, bridge resistance, or develop expressive skills include teaching the client what a feeling is, affect focusing techniques, role reversal, the alter ego exercise, the empty chair, and so forth.

Cognitive interventions: The primary goal of cognitive interventions is to "reduce emotional distress and corresponding maladaptive behavior patterns by altering or correcting errors in thoughts, perceptions and beliefs. Cognitive interventions stress the importance of self-control. Clients are viewed as the direct agents of their own changes, rather than as helpless victims of external events and forces. Illustrations of cognitive interventions include Ellis's A-B-C-D-E analysis, thought suppression, thought postponement, therapeutic paradox, and cognitive restructuring

Behavioral interventions: The overall goal of behavioral interventions is to help clients develop adaptive and supportive behaviors to multifaceted situations. Developing adaptive behavior often means helping the client weaken or eliminate behaviors that work against the desired outcome, e.g. eating snacks when you wish to lose weight. A significant part of this process involves teaching the client. Illustrative interventions include live modeling, symbolic modeling, covert modeling, role play and rehearsal, relaxation training, systematic desensitization, self-contracting and self-monitoring.

Systemic interventions: Systemic interventions are premised upon the assumption that one's environment elicits and supports the individual's dysfunctional cognitive, behavioral and affective responses. The go goal of systemic interventions is to change the individual's social environment or system, thus changing the patterns of interrelationship that elicited or supported these responses. Examples of systemic interventions (in addition to those in the preceding categories that also produce system change) include: altering communication patterns through role play and renegotiation, altering family (or system) structure by reconstructing boundaries, the family genogram, family sculpture, and providing directives for change. Children pose special issues in the selection of counseling interventions for several reasons. They have little power or control over their environment, or may lack the cognitive or affective development to respond to some interventions. For this reason, a systemic view which involves significant adults in their world often is the most effective approach to intervention selection.

Client-Centered Therapy

Client-Centered Therapy (CCT) was developed by Carl Rogers in the 40's and 50's. It is a non-directive approach to therapy, "directive" meaning any therapist behavior that deliberately steers the client in some way. The client-centered therapy, did not intend to found a school of psychotherapy with a set practice.

This theory could be used as a basis for further research on psychotherapy, and also this theory was an approximation to the truth about therapy. He did not want client-centered therapy to be "frozen" but, rather, to be a working hypothesis, a stimulus to further inquiry about the therapy process. Rogers always has been committed to promoting openness, growth and change in the pursuit of truth about therapeutic process. He has always encouraged and supported research projects and theorizing by others.

The theory in terms of attitudinal conditions, not techniques, fostered openness to different ideas about therapeutic practice. This theory left it up to the practitioner to choose which behaviors or techniques could be used to communicate the therapeutic attitudinal conditions to the client. This development in client-centered theory opened the way for practitioners from many different therapeutic schools to incorporate the basic premise and thypothesesees of attitudinal conditions into their own therapy without abandoning their original orientations. It also set the stage for the creation of a variety of new therapeutic methods based on the fundamental principles of client-centered theory.

There are many different therapy practices, and more therapies continually developing, which share the basic theory of client-centered therapy. This situation, of many evolving therapies which are often referred to as client-centered therapies, is confusing to students and confusing when one wishes to discuss differences in therapy practice with colleagues. It would clarify this situation to classify a therapy practice as a person-centered therapy whenever a therapist is trying to work from the basic hypotheses: the inherent growth principle and the major attitudinal conditions for constructive change.

There are many evolving person-centered therapies and the practice of client-centered therapy is one of those.

Client-centered therapy can be described in terms of the theory it shares with the other person-centered therapies and by its distinctive features.

The client-centered therapy is a distinctive and important practice and that it can be defined as a practice and its parameters clarified. Its evolution would be conceived within certain limits. Functioning therapeutically outside those limits would be considered, perhaps, a new and other person-centered therapy. Or someone might, also, be developing a practice outside the defined limits of the person-centered therapies. Certainly many of those already exist. The point is, this system of classification gets around the problem of freezing client-centered therapy but also permits distinctions in respect to the practices of therapy that are out there in the reality of therapeutic work.

The differences distinguishable among person-centered therapies probably make substantial differences in the experience of therapy by both client and therapist and make differences in what is observable on tapes and films and, probably, make differences in the effects of the therapy on the lives of its clients. We can study and understand these different effects much better if we distinguish practices.

The clarification and definition of client-centered therapy as distinguishable from other person-centered therapy practices can contribute to the presentation and evolution of this unique and extremely effective way of working with clients. For some time, that client-centered therapy has been misunderstood, underestimated and underused, in part, because of its ambiguities as a practice and because of its confusion with other person-centered therapeutic practices.

The central hypothesis of this approach can be briefly stated. It is that the individual has within him or her self vast resources for selfunderstanding, for altering her or his selfconcept, attitudes, and self-directed behavior--and that these resources can be tapped if only a definable climate of facilitative psychological attitudes can be provided. There are three conditions which constitute this growth-promoting climate, whether we are speaking of the relationship between therapist and client, parent and child, leader and group, teacher and student, or administrator and staff.

The conditions apply, in fact, in any situation in which the development of the person is a goal. The beliefs and hypotheses that are central to the person-centered approach are the following:

— Belief that human nature is basically constructive.

— Belief that human nature is basically social.

— Belief that self-regard is a basic human need and that self-regard, autonomy and individual sensitivity are to be protected in helping relationships.

— Belief that persons are basically motivated to perceive realistically and to pursue the truth of situations.

— Belief that perceptions are a major determinant of personal experience and behavior and, thus, to understand a person one must attempt to understand them empathically.

— Belief that the individual person is the basic unit and that the individual should be addressed, in situations intended to foster growth.

— Belief in the concept of the whole person.

— Belief that persons are realizing and protecting themselves as best they can at any given time and under the internal and external circumstances that exist at that time.

— Belief in abdication of the pursuit of control or authority over other persons and, instead, a commitment to strive to share power and control.

The basic hypothesis, the theory of therapy and the additional beliefs stated above describe the person-centered approach. These beliefs are usually shared by the people practicing the various person-centered therapies including client-centered therapy. These shared elements do not, however, distinguish client-centered therapy from the other person-centered therapies.

The salient form of client-centered therapy is the empathic understanding response process. The empathic understanding response process involves the therapist maintaining, with consistency and constancy the therapeutic attitudes in his/her experience and expressing him/herself to the client through empathic understanding responses. Empathic understanding responses are the observable responses which communicate empathic understanding to the client. They are responses intended to express and check the therapist's empathic understanding experience of the client.

In a given empathic understanding response process between therapist and client many different types of empathic understanding responses may be involved. Examples of common types oempathic understandingng responses are the following: literal responses; restatements; summaries; statements which point toward the felt experience of the client but do not name or describe the experience; interpretive or inferential guesses concerning what the client is attempting to express; metaphors; questions that strive to express understandings of ambiguious experience of the client; gestures of the therapist's face, hands, body; vocal gestures, etc.

The empathic understanding response process can appear to be very different from therapist to therapist, and between therapies with different clients by the same therapist, depending upon the types of responses which are used by the therapist.

The particular way the therapist expresses empathic understanding to the particular client does not matter, from the point of view of remaining within the client-centered framework, however, as long as the way communicates to the client the therapist's intention to understand and as long as the client feels understood by the therapist. Client-centered therapy is also distinguishable by the extreme emphasis the practice places on the non-directiveness of the therapist.

In client-centered therapy the therapist is intensely mindful to respect and protect the autonomy and self-direction of the client. The client is viewed as the expert about himself and the therapist views himself as expert only in maintaining the attitudinal conditions in the relationship with the client, not as an expert on the client. The therapeutic relationship is inherently an unequal relation in which the client is self-defined as vulnerable and in need of help and the therapist is self-defined as one who can help.

An element in the person/client-centered perspective is the belief that unequal relationships are naturally, to some extent, hurtful or harmful to the persons involved in them. Unequal relationships are sometimes necessary, for example the physician and patient or the teacher and student, because they offer desired benefits.

But the person/client-centered perspective fosters the abdication of the pursuit of power and would argue for minimizing the hurt or harm by sharing the authority as much as possible. The client-centered therapist is particularly mindful of the harmful potential side-effect of the unequal therapeutic relation and tries to share his authority as much as possible.

This awareness and effort influences all of his actions in relations to the client. Basically, the client centered therapist's view on this matter is - the authority for the client's experience is the client and the way the client uses the relationship is always left up to the client. This non-directive attitude has a significant influence on the way therapy is conducted, influencing what is done and what is not done. For example, the client-centered therapist answers client's questions.

Obviously, if the therapist decides what questions it is appropriate to answer, or takes the view that certain questions are expression of a client's avoidance of something and the therapist interprets this to help the client get on the right track, or if the therapist takes the view that the client's question is an aspect of seeking dependence on the therapist and the therapist raises this interpretation, then the therapist is acting in ways that direct the client's process.

From a client-centered viewpoint, the idea that the therapist should evaluate the desirability for the client of having his questions answered is paternalistic and an exercise of authority over the client. A client-centered therapist remains free to not answer a question asked by the client. But the reason for not answering would be explained to be a personal one - the therapist feels he does not know enough, or he feels uncomfortable in divulging the particular information, etc. - not as something that is good for the client.

There are many, many implications for the way therapy is practiced when the client-centered therapist is acting from this strongly felt attitude that the client is his own best expert and that the therapist maintain non-directiveness. The non-directive character of client-centered therapy is not only for the purpose of protecting the client's autonomy and to enhance the client's self-direction. Client-centered therapy is a fundamentally non-directive therapy because being so contributes to the distinctive therapeutic quality of the relationship between therapist and client.

This quality involves the fostering in the client of a combination of feelings - of freedom, of a positive sense of self, and of empowerment The therapist provides the basic therapeutic attitudes of congruence, acceptance and empathy. This whole way of being produces a unique experience of an authority consistently behaving in a non-authoritative manner. This abdication of the usual forms of authority carries meaning to most clients. It conveys that they are not being evaluated, not being supervised and not being controlled.

That they are not being treated in these usual ways by an authority also carries the meaning that they are being treated with respect, are being trusted, and are free, to a great extent, in the relationship. As a consequence the relationship takes on the qualities referred to above, of freedom, of enhancement of the client's sense of self and sense of personal power. Client-centered therapy is a practice in which the hypothesis of the inherent growth principle is put into action. It is also a therapy wherein the theory of therapeutic attitudes as conditions for growth is taken as the basis for functioning with the client.

It is also a therapy practice that is distinguishable by the form that it usually takes- the empathic understanding response process. It is also a therapy which emphasizes non-directiveness and wherein this principle is maximized in the relation with the client. All together, these features distinguish client-centered therapy from other extant and possible person-centered therapies.

Client-centered therapy is not the technique of "reflection of feeling" or making "empathic understanding responses". It may be useful to look at the reflection or empathic understanding responses from the point of view of technique but this should be understood as an abstraction and contrary to the spirit of their actual production. Only if empathic understanding responses, are used as expression of the therapist's genuine attitudes of congruence, acceptance and empathic understanding are they an expression of client-centered therapy. Client-centered therapy is not identical with the empathic understanding response process. This is so even though the process is the salient form of interaction in relationship of client and therapist and even though this form is one of the identifying features of client-centered therapy.

Empathic understanding response process (EURP) is not identical with the total therapy for three main reasons. First, the functions of the therapist are more than the EURP. The therapist's adaptation to the individual client as a person in a concrete relationship situation requires the application of the hypothesis and the therapeutic conditions in many ways, including the set up of the therapy, the adjustments in language for the sake of mutual understanding, and the social aspects of the therapy situation. Second, the EURP is an optimal process, as a means to express empathic understanding and express the other therapeutic attitudes to the client, for most clients who choose to engage in therapy and wish to talk about themselves and their problems.

But client-centered therapy is not limited to this population of clients. The realization of the theory of therapy with clients who do not choose therapy, or clients who are unable to talk about themselves, or clients whose illness or defects distort their relation to reality or to a relationship, may require forms of interaction which appear quite different from empathic understanding response process. Third, there are, in the usual therapy situation when EURP is the salient form, often other forms of interaction which occur in the practice. These forms, such as answering questions, giving explanations, shaping experiments for the client to try, etc., occur in and may be an integral part of a particular therapy relationship.

These forms occur in client-centered therapy, however, only when they are requested by the client or when they become the way to be with the client that gets clarified out of expressed needs or desires of the client. If forms of interaction other than EURP occur in a particular client-centered relation, the way they are expressed or done is shaped by the belief in the growth principle, the presence of the therapeutic attitudes in the therapist and the non-directiveness of the therapist.

Client-centered therapy is not based on a belief in any particular therapeutic process occurring in the client. Even if it were to be shown that the most therapeutic process in clients is a particular way of expressing the self, or a particular way of relating expression to inner experience, or particular feelings developing-toward the therapist, or a particular pattern of insights, or any other idea about how the client should act or feel or express - as the maximally therapeutic way, client-centered therapy would remain non-directive and open to the process that emerged in the client and would not involve trying to influence that process.

Client-centered therapy does not excessively restrict the therapist's resourcefulness as a helper. This is the case in two different ways. First, within the framework of client-centered therapy as defined above, it is possible for therapists, depending upon their talents and the psychotechnologies they have learned, and if they are so inclined, to utilize techniques identified with other types of therapy.

Techniques of, for example, behavioral therapy, cognitive therapy, gestalt therapy, hypnosis, focusing, relaxation, meditation, etc., may be brought into the context of ongoing client-centered therapy. But - and this is a restriction the client-centered therapy would bring these in only at the request of the client or when the interaction brings out in the client an awareness of needs that might be met by such techniques.

The client- entered therapist does not, as said before, have any convictions prior to the therapy about what process in the client, or what ways of helping, a client may need. These techniques and psychotechnologies may, then, be incorporated into a specific course of client centered therapy, as long as the therapist is not imposing them and the client is given control of the occasions and limits on their use. The second way the therapist is not restricted in the forms of help that may be given to the client is that the client-centered therapist may serve as a source of information about other therapies or treatments and as the person who helps the client utilize the therapies or treatments provided by others.

Sometimes helping the client utilize other therapies means minimizing their damage to the client that takes place as they are benefiting him. Until other helpers - physicians, psychological and behavioral therapists, psychopharmacologists, etc., are, themselves, person-centered it remains the case that many of these experts violate the self-regard or the autonomy of their patients and clients. The client-centered therapist performs a crucial service in maintaining the basic client-centered therapeutic relation while his client goes through various treatments and therapies.

These treatments may, in their specifics, be helpful to the client - even necessary - for his well-being. But without the grounding in the client-centered relation the client may be totally unable to use the services of these experts, or may be hurt or damaged in the process. In the same way that the nature of client-centered therapy, in providing optimal conditions for growth and change, facilitates the client's constructive experience of, and way of relating to, his world, it also facilitates the client's strength, confidence and good judgement in utilizing the resources of the world, including its myriad therapies, treatments and educational and remedial resources. Client-centered therapy is not inhibiting or restrictive to the natural personality of the therapist.

The therapeutic attitudinal condition of congruence the realness of the therapist, the avoidance of a role fosters the development of individuality in the therapist's presence with the client. There is a marked similarity among client-centered therapists in their shared values and in the salient form of the therapeutic relation - the empathic understanding response process. Within that form, however, the unique mind and experience of a therapist shapes his empathic grasp of the client's presented experience and shapes the specific responses that are expressed to the client.

Individuality is also expressed in the extent of personal openness and the qualities brought out in self-disclosures when they are in answer to personal questions by the client or when they are an expression of congruence. The natural personality of the therapist is generally enhanced and developed by the practice of client-centered therapy itself. The practice requires the development of the attitudinal conditions in relation to clients.

In this development, for that context, the client-centered therapist tends to develop those qualities towards himself and is, thereby self-therapeutic and self-fostering of his own individuality. Client-centered therapy is not based simply on what works. It is based on what works within the parameters of what expresses and maintains the client's experience of the attitudinal conditions and of the therapist's non-directiveness and does not contradict the presence of these conditions. The achievement of insights, or the reduction of specific symptoms, in client-centered therapy, is only considered therapeutic if it is in the context of the larger perspective of preserving the therapeutic attitudinal qualities of the relationship perceived by the client.

Client-centered therapy stems from ethical values and beliefs, even though they are held with the reservation that they are hypotheses. These values assert respect for the individual person and the belief that unconditional caring for the person is constructive for the person and also for the social milieu of the person. Whatever scientific support there may be for the client-centered theory of therapy - and there is considerable support for it, the science is not the start of the practice for the practitioner.

The foundational belief of Client Centered Therapy (CCT) is that people tend to move toward growth and healing, and have the capacity to find their own answers. This tendency is helped along by an accepting and understanding climate, which the CC therapist seeks to provide above all else. So, this is what CC therapists do:

— Listen and try to understand how things are from the client's point of view.

— Check that understanding with the client if unsure.

— Treat the client with the utmost respect and regard.

— There is also a mandate for the therapist to be "congruent", or "transparent" - which means being self-aware, self-accepting, and having no mask between oneself and the client. The therapist knows themselves and is willing to be known.

Developmental Counseling and Therapy (DCT)

Developmental counseling and therapy (DCT) is an effective strategy for conceptualizing systems theory. The counseling field has seen an increase of family counseling theories over the past 20 years. Family counseling does not refer to one specific theory, rather, it is a broad term that encompasses many theories that share similar concepts such as circular causality, cybernetic epistemology, and the importance of family interactions.

Traditional approaches to counseling, such as, psychodynamic theory, cognitive-behavioral theory, and humanistic theory, have focused on the individual. Family counseling theories do not discount the individual, but recognize that individuals live within a family, and that family has an important impact on the development of the individual. The goal of family counseling like other counseling theories is to facilitate development.

The Developmental Counseling and Therapy (DCT) theory, which is an extension or reinterpretation that addresses the sequence and process of development. DCT can be used in assessment, treatment planning, and therapy.

The general concepts of family counseling theories and DCT to form Systemic Cognitive-Developmental Therapy (SCDT). SCDT is an integrative family theory that provides an environment for facilitating family growth. It is a theoretical integration of the various family counseling theories, as well as a systemic framework for assessing the cognitive, behavioral, and emotional style of the family. SCDT does not provide any techniques; rather it relies on the counselor to integrate his/her preexisting knowledge of family counseling theories and techniques within the SCDT framework. Family Counseling and DCT Therapy theory, discuss the general concepts of family counseling theories, and provide classifications of cognitive-developmental orientations and family counseling interventions.

According to Ivey's neo-Piagetian framework, the basic principles of childhood development repeat themselves again and again in the daily lives of children, adolescents, and adults. Development is continuous, and thus developmental concepts are directly relevant to effective counseling and therapy Developmental Counseling and Therapy (DCT) is not a new form of theory, rather, it is an attempt to integrate basic developmental theory into clinical practice.

DCT focuses on the client and the holistic development of both client and counselor. Developmental Counseling and Therapy integrates counseling theory and practice in both individual and family work. DCT provides a framework that aids the counselor to assess the client's development, to help expand and change the client's view of the world, to help the counselor understand both normal and severe psychological difficulties, and to generate treatment plans.

DCT can be used as an assessment technique, a therapeutic technique, and a treatment planning tool. There are four major tenets of DCT:

(1) it is possible to assess the cognitive developmental level of a client 'on-the-spot';

(2) it then becomes possible to expand horizontal and vertical development through matching or mismatching counseling theories and methods;

(3) cognitive developmental levels facilitate different types of client

(4) a combination of the first three concepts enables the generation of a comprehensive treatment plan.

DCT maintains that counselors must enter the world of the client and understand how the client constructs their knowledge and way of being in the world. In order for the counselor to enter the world of the client, the counselor must first assess the cognitive-developmental level of the client.

Children, adolescents, and adults construct their view of the world based on four major cognitive-developmental levels, which are anchored in the Piagetian concepts of sensori-motor, concrete operations, and formal operations. In addition to the three, DCT adds the dialectic/systemic level. Each of the four levels involves varying degrees of complexity of language and meaning; however the levels are not hierarchical.

Clients operating in the sensorimotor level present themselves in a random, disorganized, confused manner, frequently jumping from topic to topic and from emotion to emotion. In the sensorimotor level, clients are able to experience their hurt and confusion fully at the body level. Clients operating from the concrete level will give concrete, linear descriptions of events, thoughts, and behaviors.

The concrete client may lack self-reflection and the ability to see multiple perspectives as well as lack the ability to generalize from situation to situation. The formal level is characterized by self-reflection and analysis of patterns of thoughts, feelings, and behaviors. The dialectic/systemic level is characterized by the integration of patterns of thoughts and emotions into a system.

After assessing the cognitive-developmental level of the client, the counselor can choose appropriate interventions and theories either to match or to mismatch the cognitive-developmental level of the client. Horizontal development occurs when the counselor helps the client expand their understanding at their current cognitive-developmental level, thus helping the client develop all of the resources of the stage at which he or she is operating.

For example, if a sensorimotor functioning client enters counseling, it is important to match the client at the sensorimotor level and expand sensorimotor functioning before moving the client to concrete and formal understanding. Vertical development involves the counselor shifting styles to move the client to the other levels of development, thus helping the client expand developmental potential.

For example, after the counselor has helped the sensorimotor functioning client expand sensorimotor functioning, the counselor mismatches the client and helps the client move towards concrete understanding. Regardless of where the counselor begins with the client, the objective of counseling is to help the client move through the different developmental levels.

Effective counseling produces both horizontal and vertical development, thus helping the client explore and develop resources in each of the developmental levels.

The counselor's cognitive-developmental level greatly influences the manner in which the client replies. Clients will talk about what the counselor attends to and clients will talk and act at the cognitive-developmental level at which the counselor listens, asks questions, and conducts the session.

Using specific questions focusing on one of the cognitive levels, the counselor can help the client explore their issue at each cognitive-developmental level. Whether the counselor chooses to use the DCT model in assessment, treatment planning, and/or therapy, it is important to remember that central to DCT is the idea of co-construction.

The counselor and the client are co-constructing the nature of the relationship and the goals of counseling throughout the counseling process. DCT provides an integrative approach to understanding individual development; however, it does not consider the individual within the family context. It is apparent that individuals live in a family. One cannot discuss the development of the individual without discussing the family.

General Family Counseling

Family counseling is not one specific form of theory but a broad term that encompasses many theories. The counseling field has seen an explosion of family counseling theories and interventions making it impossible to cover each in detail. In 1982, Grunebaum and Chasin present a classification system, which assumes that families can be seen from three different perspectives, historical, interactional, and existential. The various family theories may differ in some aspects; however, all of them share a systemic worldview. In other words, general systems theory serves as the foundation of all family counseling theories.

General systems theory concludes the following:

1) elements of a system are organized and predictable,
2) families behave in a stable and predictable manner,
3) families are able to change as situations dictate

4) the family forms a single entity with its own characteristics,
5) family members are bounded by time and space,
6) hierarchies exist within families,
7) families seek homeostasis, and
8) families function according to feedback loops, by which individual family members influence the family and the family influences the individuals

In short, the following general concepts appear to be a part of most family theories:

1) the family is the primary unit,
2) the family influences the individual,
3) the individual influences the family,
4) the family consists of subsystems,
5) every event within the family is determined by multiple forces operating within the system/ subsystem,
6) families form repetitive patterns over time,
7) family members have family roles,
8) family is viewed in terms of interactions and relationships, and
9) the focus of family counseling is on the family system

Because family systems are made up of individuals, it makes sense to integrate the concepts of DCT discussed earlier with the general concepts of family counseling theories in discussing the development and functioning of families.

Systemic Cognitive-Developmental Therapy (SCDT) combines the general concepts of DCT and family counseling theories to form an integrative theory that emphasizes the importance of providing a therapeutic environment that promotes family growth. SCDT proposes that families collectively move through cognitive-developmental orientations similar to the DCT levels. The cognitive-developmental orientations within SCDT include the sensorimotor family, the concrete-operational family, the formal-operational family, and the dialectic/systemic family. Families repeatedly progress through the four cognitive-developmental orientations over the life-time and families can become stuck and immobilized in one orientation.

Families tend to frame a specific issue in one orientation. Although families can operate on all four levels, they tend to have a preferred orientation. Families develop a collective worldview that organizes predictable ways of thinking, feeling, and acting that are anchored in one of the four orientations. The family uses its primary mode of operating to filter the way in which it views the world. A counselor can assess the cognitive-developmental orientation of the family through listening and utilizing a questioning sequence.

Families must be able to either integrate new situations and emotions into their existing worldview or modify their existing worldview to fit the new situation or emotion. Thus, a functional family can cope with new situations and emotions from their preferred orientation and also from each of the other orientations.

Dysfunctional families tend to choose extreme methods of integrating new situations and emotions. They hold strongly to their preferred orientation and are unable to move and operate under the other orientations. The role of the counselor in SCDT is very similar to the role of the counselor in DCT.

The counselor must first assess the cognitive-developmental orientation of the family, including any blocks, and then co-construct with the family the therapeutic relationship and goals. Ultimately, the goal of SCDT is to assist family to functioning within and among the four cognitive-developmental orientations, to empower the family to view their issues from multiple perspectives, and to generate solutions that are appropriate for the developmental needs of the family.

Similarly to DCT, SCDT begins the counseling process with a structured interview that identifies the family's cognitive-developmental orientation. Once the family's orientation has been identified, the counselor creates an environment helping the family use multiply orientations to explore different perspectives of the presenting issue. As in DCT, SCDT encourages change through horizontal movement, where the counselor helps the family elaborate and explore resources at their current orientation of functioning, and/or vertical movement, where the counselor helps the family move to and function at the other cognitive-developmental orientations.

SCDT does not offer new techniques beyond the specific questioning sequence, family counselors must use the techniques of other family counseling theories within the SCDT framework. Many interventions fit into multiple orientations. It is the intentional use by the counselor that determines the influence of the intervention on the family. For example, the genogram activity can be used to help the family identify interpersonal closeness, to organize family information (concrete-operational), to analyze repeating patterns, and to bring to awareness cultural and intergenerational influences.

Sensorimotor orientation Interventions that either match or help the client family move to the sensorimotor orientation include: genogram, family photos, family sculpture, unbalancing techniques, art therapy, and dance and movement therapy. A genogram provides a graphic picture of the family history over at least three generations.

The genogram can be used to reveal the family's basic structure, demographics, functioning, and relationships. A SCDT counselor can use the genogram activity to expand or move the family into the sensorimotor orientation by focusing on feelings the family is experiencing while creating the genogram and discussing family interactions. The family photo technique involves having family members bring in family albums, photos, slides, or videos and having family members discuss the emotional significance of the events or what feeling each family member is experiencing as they reflect on the picture.

Family sculpture is a re-creation of the family system that represents relationships to one another at a specific period in time. The family is asked to sculpt their family by physically arranging the family, paying attention to distancing and body positions. The counselor can use family sculpture to elicit powerful feelings from the family during the sculpting and afterwards as they discuss the final product.

The counselor purposefully chooses to side with one family member, creating a disequilibrium with the hopes that the other family members will emotionally respond to the disequilibrium. Counselors can use art therapy techniques to have family members draw images of their family or have family members jointly draw their family.

The counselor can help the family explore their feelings about their drawing as well as their feelings about the drawings of other family members. Art therapy can be used to encourage relatedness among family members as well as to stimulate expression of emotions. Concrete-operational orientation Interventions that either match or help the client family move to the concrete-operational orientation include: genogram, family sculpture, homework assignments, "going home" technique, miracle question, fast forwarding questioning, communication skills training, and exceptions to the problem.

The process of constructing a family genogram can help expand either the concrete-operational family or it can help move a family to the concrete-operational orientation. Organizing family information such as, putting names and dates on the symbols, and delineating family relationships can be a very concrete activity. Family sculpting, like the genogram, can be very concrete-operational. The task of creating the family sculpture, arranging the body position of various family members, and distancing the family members can be a very concrete task.

Homework assignments, the "going home technique" which involves having the client return to his/her family of origin and record interactions between family members, the use of the miracle question, and fast forwarding questions, and communication skills training, all help the client family explore or move into the concrete-operational orientation. These interventions help the client family organize family information, form concrete, tangible responses to specific questions and assignments, and provide straightforward directives for the family members to carry out.

Formal-operational orientation Interventions that either match or help the client family move to the formal-operational orientation include: genogram, family sculpture, reframing, relabeling, and "going home" technique. The genogram can be used to help explore family patterns. Throughout the genogram activity, the counselor can ask questions that will direct the family to look for and analyze family patterns. Like the genogram, the family sculpture can also help analyze family patterns. The counselor can help the family discuss the different relationships that are evident in the family sculpture.

Each family member and the counselor may view situations and behaviors differently. Although the family members share a common background, there are other outside influences on the individual family member that contribute to the individual's unique development. The combination of family and outside influences results in the development of an individual with his/her own way of thinking, behaving, and feeling. There are many other family counseling interventions that can be adapted into the SCDT framework. The specific intervention is not as important as the manner in which the counselor intentionally chooses to use the interventions. Many interventions can be used in multiple orientations. It is up to the skilled, intentional counselor to decide what intervention to use when, and how to use the intervention that would be the most beneficial for the family.

Therapy model and family counseling theories naturally fit together to form Systemic Cognitive-Developmental Therapy, a family counseling theory that places the general concepts of family/systems theory within the DCT framework. SCDT provides an alternative paradigm for the assessment, treatment, and conception of family issues that builds on preexisting family counseling theories and techniques. Although SCDT does not offer any new interventions, it does provide a framework for using the existing interventions in a new context.

When the counselor asks the family to construct a genogram, the counselor is not merely asking for a family tree. Within the SCDT model, the counselor can use the genogram to understand the preferred orientation of functioning for each of the family member and the family as a whole. Additionally, the counselor can have the family members think about the preferred orientation of functioning for other family members on the genogram to facilitate communication and understanding among the various family members.

The SCDT model provides an innovative and integrative theory of family counseling that does not discount other family counseling theories but provides a framework that recognizes the importance of the various perspectives within each of the four orientations. Although many interventions can be used in multiple orientations, there are some interventions associated with certain family counseling theories that appear to fit better with one particular orientation.

For example, mediation, body work, and gestalt approaches to family counseling appear to fit nicely within the sensorimotor orientation. Behavioral, reality therapy, problem-solving, strategic, solution-focused, and structural approaches to family counseling can be most helpful within the concrete-operational orientation.

Cognitive, client-centered, structural, psycho-dynamic, and constructivism approaches to family counseling align nicely with the formal-operational orientation.

Feminist theory, cultural identity theory, and most family counseling theories will help the counselor in the dialectic/systemic orientation. The SCDT model of family counseling is an advanced theory, which may intimidate beginning counselors. SCDT provides no clear direction but a framework for the counselor to build on.

Although SCDT provides an excellent framework that will easily aid the counselor in assessing the family's preferred orientation and blocked orientations, it provides no additional information to assist the counselor in choosing the appropriate intervention other than suggesting either horizontal or vertical movement. A counselor-in-training or novice counselor may know that the best intervention for the client family is to match the client family at the sensorimotor orientation; however, within the sensorimotor orientation, the counselor may not know enough about the various interventions to choose a genogram, movement therapy, or a gestalt approach.

The SCDT's reliance on counselors to use the techniques of other family counseling theories within the SCDT framework assumes that counselors already have knowledge of other counseling theories and techniques which may not be true for counselors-in-training or novice counselors. The SCDT model can be very helpful for advanced family counseling counselors who already have many intervention skills in their repertoire. However, for counselors-in-training and novice counselors who are just beginning to learn family counseling interventions, the idea of coming up with a number of interventions to help the family move along the orientations can be somewhat overwhelming. Overall, the SCDT model is a theory of family counseling, which provides a theoretical framework for counselors to understand their client family within a developmental perspective.

Multifamily Group Psychotherapy

Family therapists have long understood the complications in assessing and influencing a single family system. To assess several families and manage process between and among families simultaneously presents a considerable task. Yet, multifamily group therapy, combining group psychotherapy and theory and technique from family therapy, has the potential for significant treatment efficacy. Multifamily groups are a valuable treatment modality and provide a powerful medium for change. The curative factors within the group process and the reenactment of family issues in family therapy are only a few of the important reasons that make multifamily groups effective. For family therapists, a general systems model of treatment encourages this therapeutic approach. Combining techniques from both therapy models provide a wealth of interventions and resources from which the therapist can use to help their clients. MFG also allows the advantages of family therapy --seeing the family together, access to the dysfunctional patterns, and the therapeutic material from the family to be seen in the context of a group situation involving similar difficulties across families.

Multifamily groups (MFG) began as a adjunct to planned hospital treatment and has historically been linked with the education of family members concerning various presenting problems related to the patient who was hospitalized. Yet, most definitions now include a wider view of the multifamily group that can be adopted to outpatient and other treatment settings. O'Shea and Phelps provide the following definition of MFG:

> "...a deliberate, planful, psychosocial intervention with two or more families present in the same room with a trained therapist for all or most of the sessions. Each participating family should have two or more members that represent at least two generations in the family and are present for all or most of the sessions. Sessions should have an explicit focus on problems or concerns shared by all families in attendance"

They report that the focal problems of the group should pertain directly or indirectly to cross-generational family interaction. The sessions should reflect interfamilial and intergenerational interaction. Also, actual or potential alliances among members of different families based on similarities can be utilized to achieve group goals. Lacqueur is generally quoted by writers in this area as the first to attempt to combine family and group treatment. Lacqueur writes that only in this modality was society present in the form of several, unrelated family units. The larger, external influencing system was seen as having stronger, richer and more varied resources for change than group or family therapy alone. Thus, MFG has been described in the literature as a distinct hybrid that grew out of needs within institutions and their pragmatic concerns for providing efficient therapeutic treatment and a combination of group and family work.

MFG can be found in a wide variety of institutions, private agencies and among individuals providing therapy. A review of the literature reveals use with a large range of client populations including: schizophrenics, bulimics, learning disabilities, behavioral problems, mentally challenged, severely disturbed psychiatric populations, and adolescent substance abuse. However, it would appear that many family and interpersonal issues, yet to be addressed, could utilize multifamily group therapy. The multifamily group leader(s) must possess clinical expertise and have training in assessment, treatment, and evaluation in order to be effective.

While many disciplines are represented in the literature on MFG, the proficient leader, regardless of training program, must have a thorough knowledge of group therapy including group dynamics and development and competencies in family psychotherapy. Knowledge in the various schools of family therapy including: structural/strategic; inter generational; Bowenian, solution-focused, and psychodynamic is helpful. For the most part, the structure of the MFG varies with the setting in which the group leader works. In general, MFGs are composed of three or more families gathering to discuss common concerns. Lacqueur originally recommended that groups be heterogeneous in SES, and other characteristics, so that the group would focus on relationship issues.

The structure of the group refers to the process of establishing the type of group, planning, per-group interviews, beginning, middle and termination, and follow-up stages. First, a rationale for establishing a multifamily group must take into account several factors: the issues and the common concern for the group;

whether it be an open or closed group; how often and for how long will it meet; what type of family will benefit from the group; and group leadership. Pre-group interviews are important to facilitate orientation to the therapy model and to set expectations for membership. It also provides an opportunity for pretesting family functioning and allows for a subjective test of compatibility between families.

There are at least three distinctive phases or stages that structure the multifamily group process. The first stage is characterized by education of the members about the group intent. As with most groups, this phase involves settling in and establishing group norms and purpose. During this stage, the therapist is active and provides a good deal of structure emphasizing similarities between family goals and circumstances. Family members are encouraged to interact with each other within their own family and the therapist intervenes to model and promote constructive interactions. This gives the families time to adapt to their surroundings before demands are placed on them. Discussion may also lead to the group's relationship to other environmental systems, i.e., school system, courts, etc. as the group becomes an entity.

In the middle stage, the therapist interaction and direction decreases. Interventions become more selective. Intra-family interaction occurs spontaneously. The interfamily process increases and the therapist's linking of intra-family peers may decrease. Families may report that contact outside the group is occurring. For the multifamily group, this networking can be positive. Group rules set prior to this may help to prevent splitting or the type of subgrouping that is detrimental to group process.

Therapists continue to assess family relationships: what triangles are occurring, what distorted perceptions are there, sequential behavior patterns, family myths, and a measure of family flexibility and resolve to change. During this middle phase, spotlighting one family to work can be beneficial. This assessment will allow the therapist to intervene appropriately as intra- and interfamily problems arise. The processing of a particular issue may involve participation from all group members.

The ending stage allows for the gains and understandings from past sessions to be discussed, so that the group begins to end on a positive note and gains may be reinforced. Here, the therapist begins to take on a more directive role again. The intra-family process consists of review for each family and the discussion of expectations for the future.

In general, the family therapy techniques, fit well in the Multifamily Group model. Techniques associated with imagery and fantasy, structural exercises, family problem-solving, psychodrama, role-play, genogram drawings, behavioral contracting, and intergenerational homework are well adapted for MFG. Imagery work including guided visual imagery and relaxation techniques are also suited to MFG. Other techniques such as: early recollections, recall of early years, and empty chair techniques are extremely valuable. Roles such as fathers, mothers, teenagers, children, the targeted or symptom group, oldest, youngest, etc., that naturally occur in families can be included in structured exercises during the MFG. Structural family therapy techniques provide an opportunity for changes in perspectives. For example, family sculpting and family portraits are interesting and fun exercises for the participants. Strategic interventions, while well-suited for individual families, may be inadvisable due to compatibility issues across families in the group. Importantly, the processing of the results of these techniques becomes an most important component of the group work.

Impact Therapy and Group Counseling

Impact Therapy is a concrete approach to group leading with much emphasis on the leader leading the group. A number of different models of group counseling exist that tend to put much of the responsibility for the outcome of the group on the members rather than the leader. The emphasis of these models has been on the interpersonal dynamics or group process rather than on the intrapersonal experience of each individual.

The Impact Therapy approach to group leading puts more emphasis on the individual's needs and how the leader can make the group experience valuable for each member. Impact Therapy is an active, multi-sensory approach to counseling that encourages the leader to be creative by using props, chairs, movement, writing and drawing to tap into members' different learning styles.

Impact Therapy integrates creative counseling techniques and ideas from RET, TA, Gestalt Therapy, Reality Therapy, Adlerian Therapy. It stresses listening, thinking, action, and impact, whereas many other approaches primarily emphasize listening and facilitating. Impact Therapy group leaders are guided by the following four core beliefs:

1. People don't mind being led when they are led well.
2. Group counseling should be clear and concrete.
3. Group counseling should never be boring.

4. The leader is primarily responsible for what happens in a group session.

The impact therapist uses the initials PPFF (purpose, plan, focus, funnel) as the primary organizing "map" for setting up and conducting a group session.

— *Purpose.* The leader is very clear as to the kind of group (educational, support, counseling, or therapy) and why the group is meeting.

— *Plan.* The impact therapist always plans the session. Good planning of the warm-up, middle, and closing phases is essential and yet many leaders do not plan or plan superficially. In-depth planning helps greatly in making group sessions productive.

— *Focus.* The Impact Therapy group leader consciously focuses the session; that is, sees to it that relevant topics or issues are discussed. One of the biggest problems in groups is that the session never focuses long enough for there to be impact. Without focus, members go from topic to topic, causing the interaction to be superficial or disjointed. Unfortunately many leaders have been trained to wait for the members to focus the session.

— *Funnel.* The impact therapist is always thinking of how to funnel the session; that is, how to take the session to a deeper, more meaningful level. Impact Therapy leaders feel that it is their responsibility to funnel the session. Funneling is accomplished by asking good thought-provoking questions, by using deepening exercises, or by working with an individual using theory and the other members. Sessions have much more impact when they are funneled and often sessions will not funnel unless the leader actively intervenes and directs the group.

The impact therapist believes that funneling is the key to a successful group.

The Impact Therapy group leader has the courage and permission to do what it takes to make a session productive. The leader is willing to take the session to a meaningful level by using counseling theory, psychodrama, the other members, or him or herself in whatever way that may have impact on the members. The leader is willing to draw out and cut off members when it is appropriate to do so. In order to focus and funnel a session, the leader often will need to interrupt and redirect the flow of conversation. Cutting off is an essential skill for group leading. Leaders whc allow members to be inappropriate, ramble, distract the group, or tell long, detailed stories are not being as effective as they can be.

Creative techniques

Using creative activities is an integral part of being an Impact Therapy group leader. Creative techniques help make the group session more engaging, interesting, and meaningful. There are a number of creative techniques that have been useful in groups.

— *Large Newsprint Pad or Wipeboard.* Many people are visual learners. The benefit of having something large to write on cannot be over emphasized. It is helpful to visually represent concepts or ideas to the group such as irrational and rational self-talk, lists generated by the members, time lines, TA drawings, or drawings of enmeshment.

— *Use of Movement.* The Impact Therapy group leader often has members stand up and move around to make points more concrete or to generate energy in the group. Group exercises that involve movement are valuable. Having members "sculpt" how they feel about the group or move along a "progress" line as to how much they have progressed, or move along value continuums are excellent movement exercises. Having members move between chairs that represent different people, ego states, or goals can serve as a valuable visual and experiential learning activity. Physical movement can be very beneficial in groups.

— *Small Child's Chair.* Another essential tool for Impact Therapy group leaders is a small child's chair which can be used in a variety of ways. The chair can be used to represent the Child ego state or the little boy or girl in each of the members. So often, when a member is struggling with an issue, part of the problem has to do with the child part of themselves. The small chair makes the struggle more concrete for members. Having members sit in the chair or even look at the chair can be quite impactful.

— *Shield.* The impact therapist often will use a prop (some tangible item such as a shield, cup, filter, rubber band, or blocks) for an exercise or when working with an individual member. Frequently members talk about needing to shield themselves from verbal abuse from someone in their lives such as a parent, spouse, or boss. By having them hold a shield as they discuss how they need to protect themselves, the members get the point about how they can make themselves safe.

— *Other Props.* Styrofoam cups are used to represent one's self-worth. Punching holes in the cup to indicate "leaks in self-esteem" or smashing the cup to represent how members allow themselves to be psychologically smashed are two ways that cups can be used. A furnace filter is a good prop for getting members to discuss how they may need to filter input from certain people in their lives. Rubber bands can be used regarding stress--each person can stretch the rubber band to the level of stress they are feeling and then discuss either adding to the stress or reducing the stress. Wooden blocks with holes in them and pegs that either fit in the holes or nearly fit, or definitely do not fit can be used to symbolize the "fit" of relationships in members' lives.

Group Counseling for older personalities

Declining birth and infant mortality rates have combined with increased longevity to create an expanding population of older persons. Individually and collectively, the developmental task is to continue realizing the full potential, self-actualizing, and being fully functional. The counseling profession is challenged to help older persons and their caregivers influence society to create and maintain an environment in which ego integrity, empowerment, and meaning are not only possible, but probable. Group counselors can contribute in seemingly small but significant ways by offering groups which are small models of a larger world. They can teach older persons how to cope with a new and often difficult stage of development.

For older persons a major challenge is to traverse their graying years with a sense of ego integrity, empowerment, and meaning. The ultimate developmental task of ego integrity is marked by satisfaction with a life well spent, and the absence of despair or discouragement. Empowerment is the ability to develop positive, satisfying lifestyles and maximize developmental potential and life satisfaction. Meaning may be found in core values and themes, or a sense of continuity. Although many individuals spend most of their older years in good mental and physical health, sound financial status, and with a solid family and social support system, aging is inevitably accompanied by loss.

Increased vulnerability to health problems may create financial difficulties and unwelcomed lifestyle changes, resulting in loss of autonomy. The illness or death of a spouse and cohorts may render the healthiest older person fearful, alienated and lonely. Feelings of worthlessness may develop as older individuals internalize their devalued social position and lose control over their lives. The normal losses of aging are intensified for homebound or institutionalized older adults suffering serious mental and physical impairment.

Resisting discouragement and despair may become difficult for older persons coping with multiple losses. Feeling empowered and finding meaning may seem impossible in the face of alienation and isolation. If the challenge for aging persons is to transcend these obstacles to ego integrity, empowerment and meaning, the challenge for society is to create an environment where the effects of such obstacles are minimized. Groups for older persons and their caregivers can provide small but developmentally healthy environments where the losses associated with aging may be translated into gains.

Several types of groups for older people are described in the literature, each having benefits common to most groups, and benefits specific to the particular type of group. Developmental benefits common to most groups include

(a) increased feelings of community and belonging,

(b) strengthened social support and interaction,

(c) decreased isolation and loneliness,

(d) acquired coping skills,

(e) rediscovered uniqueness,

(f) resolved issues, and

(g) restored sense of control, self-worth and integrity.

Reminiscing groups are appropriate for older persons living independently in the community and functional older persons in long-term care facilities. These life review groups are especially helpful for finding order and affirmation in the patterns of one's life and in discovering central meanings in seemingly disconnected parts of life. Resolving past hurts and conflicts, discovering core values, and identifying personal themes help members find meaning from their past. Training groups may provide a safe environment in any setting for learning new coping skills to deal with losses. Participants can also learn interpersonal skills to develop new friendships, repair relationships, and rebuild a needed but weakened support network.

Psychotherapy groups in community or institutional settings help members with diminished coping skills adjust to life stresses and personal problems. Reality orientation groups are usually conducted in inpatient settings and are more appropriate for older persons disoriented in time and place. Preventing and slowing progressive deterioration are goals of this group type.

Additional benefits from a variety of groups are apparent in the group titles, such as remotivation, exercise, bereavement, assertiveness, family therapy, sexuality, self-esteem, or art, music and psychodrama groups. Groups for caregivers of older persons can help make the older person's environment developmentally healthy and conducive to empowerment. Caregivers experience problems with confinement, infringement on lifestyle, restricted social life, work and family conflicts, and emotional and physical stress. Groups can help caregivers reduce conflict and stress, deal with special parental needs, increase understanding of illnesses, and use available resources. When caregivers find information, resources, and support, they are able to significantly improve the environment of older family members. A group growing in popularity is the peer group. Seniors counseling seniors may be empathic, respectful and without the negative attitudes toward working with older persons reported of many professionals. Peer group counselors may also provide empowered role models for successful aging.

Counselors offering groups for older persons need the basic knowledge and competency skills recommended by the Association for Specialists in Group Work (ASGW). Counselors should also have specific training in developmental issues of aging, effects of various physical or mental limitations, intergenerational issues, common aging concerns, and resources available for older persons. Specific counseling skills needed for psychotherapy or reality orientation groups differ from those skills needed for reminiscing or training groups. Family therapy, art, music and drama, sexuality or other specialized groups would each require specific competencies in addition to general group and gerontological competencies. An ideal training format might be a combination of the Council for Accreditation of Counseling and Related Educational Programs (CACREP) gerontology speciality program and a formal counselor education program adhering to both CACREP standards and the ASGW standards for training group counselors. A counselor graduating from a program not approved by CACREP or a program not following the ASGW professional standards could plan an individualized training supplement to acquire the equivalent of the ideal training format. Caution is encouraged when advocating peer group counseling with older persons. Waters and Goodman emphasized the necessity of carefully selecting peer group counselors, and providing training that is skill oriented. Paraprofessional skills are rarely as developed as those of professional counselors.

Philosophical counselling

Philosophical counselling, following Achenbach, is essentially a method "beyond-method". It is not doctrinally committed, but rather is a philosophically informed dialogical practice, which enables individuals to explore their hopes, fears and anxieties within a setting which is likely to promote deeper self-understanding. What unites philosophical counsellors is their rejection of the excesses of the medical-model and their insistence that it is normal for a person to have psychological issues that need to be addressed. And herein lies a problem. There are no criteria generally accepted by philosophical counsellors which determine whether a psychological problem is susceptible to philosophical practice or not. Lets take schizophrenia as an example.

In its more severe manifestations, schizophrenia is characterised by: delusions (paranoia or grandeur); hallucinations; incoherent thought; disassociation from reality; flat emotions; and so on. It is normally treated by means of anti-psychotic drugs, which function to inhibit dopamine (a neurotransmitter) activity in the brain. But is there a role for philosophical counselling in the treatment of schizophrenia? Philosophical counsellors should not treat severe personality disorders, and presumably schizophrenia is included amongst their number. However, things are not quite this straightforward.

— It is not clear what kind of therapy a philosophical counsellor can recommend to a client who presents the symptoms of schizophrenia. Many philosophical counsellors reject the medical model completely, but anti-psychotic drugs, which have a direct and measurable somatic effect, have transformed the lives of many schizophrenics over the last 30 years.

— Perhaps more disturbingly,

Philosophical counsellors who endeavour to treat everything by philosophical means. They are deconstructed enough themselves to have taken what evidence the undermining of absolutism and to have applied it to the other extreme. Of course, many of them are scientifically semi-literate and they suppose, for example, that the theory of relativity proves that everything is relative (they say as much in their literature). They will then attempt to solve all sorts of problems by philosophical means that might not be philosophical problems. Of course, every therapeutic and mental health discipline will have its fair share of practitioners who perhaps should not be practising. But there is specific problem for philosophical counselling—and it is the problem of relativism. Because philosophical counselling lacks a delimited method and conceptual framework, the boundaries of acceptable practice are likely to remain fluid.

Consequently, it is unlikely that there will ever be a formal set of guidelines that specify which kinds of problems are philosophical in nature and which are not. If these guidelines do not exist, then there will always be philosophical counsellors who are willing to deal with disorders such as schizophrenia, which would be better handled by the medical profession. Moreover, this relativism extends also to the content of philosophical counselling. It is difficult to see, for example, why a philosophical counsellor could not encourage a religiously informed discourse to address the problems of schizophrenia. Or perhaps a discourse informed by Jungian concepts or Eastern philosophy.

It might be thought that this is not really a problem. Different people will have different preferences, in terms of what they want from a counsellor. However, this is to fail to recognise that many psychological problems can be very effectively handled by specific and established therapeutic programmes. For instance, embark on a programme of systematic desensitisation, because it works. In the first instance, visit a philosopher. The "horses for courses" view also suggests the relativism that Roger Scruton finds so repugnant. To be cavalier about the content of philosophical counselling seems to deny that philosophy has a privileged role to play in the pursuit of truth.

So the problem of relativism is not, that individual philosophical counsellors articulate their philosophies to the needs of their clients. It is rather that philosophical counselling as an institution is ambivalent about method and content. Consequently, it fails to specify either the kinds of issues that can be addressed by philosophical practice or the sorts concepts and methods that should be employed in the endeavour. In this "anything-goes" sense, philosophical counselling is suggestive of a post-modern phenomenon.

The open-ended character of philosophical counselling methodology confers enormous responsibility on counsellors for the well-being of their clients. Consequently, their credibility and integrity is absolutely essential. Indeed, more so than is the case in psychotherapy and psychiatry, where practitioners can follow clearly established methods, arguably regardless of their own personal qualities. The confident about the credibility and integrity of philosophical counsellors? In some ways, it is easy to see why a philosopher might make a good personal counsellor. For example, the ability to listen and to respond rationally is clearly essential to the task of counselling a couple with marital difficulties. And similarly, a background in ethics will be useful in aiding a woman to come to a decision with regard to her unwanted pregnancy. But one must not be carried away by such examples, for it is just as easy to construct instances which demonstrate the absurdity of philosophers as counsellors. For example, it is hard to imagine why a background in formal logic or the philosophy of science will help a philosopher deal with obsessive-compulsive disorder. And similarly, it seems unlikely that the poker waving Wittgenstein would have been particularly successful in aiding a man to control his violent temper. Of course, these kinds of examples will be dismissed as "straw-men" by the advocates of philosophical counselling. They will respond that it is a certain kind of philosophical training that lends credibility to the idea that philosophers will make good counsellors. And further that it is possible to ensure the high-standard of philosophical counselling by instituting programmes of official certification. But these responses are not adequate. The other standard response to the charge that philosophers lack credibility as counsellors is to point to the short-comings of psychology and psychiatry. It is the 'psychotherapy in crisis' response. But again it is not satisfactory.

In the first place, it is flawed logically. The alleged shortcomings of established therapies are no justification for instituting another kind of flawed therapy. If anything the opposite is the case. But perhaps more importantly, the "psychotherapy in crisis" response is disingenuous about the successes of the mental-health disciplines. Consider that prior to the 1950s, schizophrenia was thought untreatable, patients were confined to mental institutions and their wards were termed "snake pits". But with phenothiazine drugs many sufferers are now able to live relatively normal lives in the community. And successes are not restricted to the somatic treatments: behavioural therapies are very effective in dealing with specific anxieties and addictions; and cognitive-behavioural therapies are fruitful in treating depression, anxiety disorders and sexual dysfunction. Indeed, if philosophical counsellors are able to duplicate the successes of the established disciplines, they will be doing well.

8

Ethical and Legal Aspects of Guidance Counselling

The field of counselling has been moving towards a more self-confident professional status, in the past few years. There are many aspects of this process which are to be welcomed - not least because it helps to enhance the credibility of counsellors working in a variety of settings. The counselling and psychotherapy more and more pushed towards a purely surface-oriented, symptom-focused and cost-driven approach. The psychotherapy that has adopted the market approach par excellence is behaviour therapy. The practice of graded exposure to phobic stimuli incorporates the routine measurement of symptoms during treatment and the recording of hours of therapy.

Recent issues of counselling have contained strongly expressed arguments in favour of the growth of research, audit and evaluation in the field of counselling has also argued for counsellors taking an increasing interest in evaluation and audit. Potential employers will want harder evidence and it is likely that counsellors will be required to provide such evidence in the not too distant future. counsellor training courses will need to put evaluation and audit on the curricula. There can be a seductive fascination and excitement with the world of seemingly 'objective' statistical techniques. One of the greatest dangers of predominantly or exclusively quantitative research is that we end up knowing the price (or numerical value) of everything, and the value (or essential quality) of nothing.

The desire to quantify, irrespective of the appropriateness of such an approach to the subject matter under consideration, is one which has to be self-consciously and tirelessly guarded against - for the seductive power of quantification, and the appeal that it makes to the scientistic, technocratic mind at this point in the evolution of human consciousness, is such that we can so easily be seduced into entirely inappropriate research procedures without even realising it. Anyone of humanistic persuasion who is familiar with the empirical research literature in any of the social sciences (including many branches of the psychology discipline) can only surely wince at the aridity and disembodied irrelevance of a significant proportion of the conventional literature in the academic journals.

The dynamics of the global social system are driven by shared, species-wide developmental traumata which are normally repressed from awareness, and the effects of which only tend overtly to manifest themselves dysfunctionally under conditions of high stress and anxiety, and diminishing resources. Some study describes that the objectivist epistemology of empiricist methodology, and its associated zeal for quantification, can be understood in this light; and that it is only through the experiential task of working through and integrating the repressed and unintegrated material of early developmental experience that we will be in a position individually and collectively to heal our individual and collective psychic dis-integration and move towards a wholeness from which it is far more likely that an epistempology and methodology which is truly humanistic in nature will organically emerge.

There are inherent difficulties in any attempt to fashion a meaningful understanding of existence in terms of the moral and epistemological categories provided by scientific culture. The increasing attention being given to qualitative research will... help to introduce reluctant counsellors to the world of research as it is... more in keeping with the spirit of counselling than quantitative research. There is, further, a substantial literature on qualitative research philosophy and methodology; and the pioneering volume edited by John Rowan and Peter Reason on 'new paradigm research' provides an excellent base from which to develop the kinds of sensitive, person-centred research on which a humanistic evaluation practice should surely be based.

The quantifying methodology is the appropriate approach for evaluating the efficacy of humanistic-dynamic counselling; yet the kinds of factors that a humanistic perspective holds to be decisive in facilitating therapeutic change represent human qualities that are quite beyond the ambit of controlled and 'objective' scientific measurement and mechanistic modes of understanding. The positivist scientific practices, which place such emphasis on the principles of falsifiability, replicability, predictability and substitutability, are quite inappropriate for studying the human psyche and the therapeutic change process. There has been an almost 'intentional blindness' within the psychology discipline to the conditions of production of psychological knowledge. Any counselling training or degree course which is advocating or insisting upon its trainees or students carrying out research into counselling would do well to leave considerable space for reflection upon the dynamics of the research process itself - focusing on both the researcher's own particular personality dynamics in so far as they resonate with and determine the choice of research methodology, and also the wider cultural dynamics and ideology of modernity which underlie orthodox and received research practice.

Academic departments in counselling, counselling psychology and psychotherapy should surely pay close and attentive heed to the 'conditions of production' of research knowledge, if the kind of sterile and disembodied empiricism described earlier is to be avoided. There is also a steadily growing body of literature in the psychology field which offers a potentially devastating critique of empirical social-scientific research from the post-modernist standpoint. Anyone who is concerned to promulgate and advocate research-mindedness in the counselling field should at the very least be fully aware of the post-modernist challenge to empiricism, and be prepared and able to offer a coherent and sustainable response to the formidable post-modernist critique.

Some commentators are rightly concerned that a full embracing of the 'anti-epistemology' of post-modernist thinking might lead to a sort of formless relativism in which we end up in a solipsistic position where it is impossible to say anything about the world beyond the subjective and purely private. Perhaps post-modernism is a kind of 'reaction-formation' against the excesses of the soul-less scientism of modernity; and it seems to me that the fields of counselling and psychotherapy are in a unique position to develop an embodied, humanistic approach to research that transcends the ideology of objectivism, and which honours both our need for communicable inter-subjective knowledge about the world and our core humanistic principles, which elevate the values of holism and human meaning above those of mechanism and quantifiability.

Ethical and Legal Aspetcs of Counselling

The process of determining which ethical principles are involved and then prioritizing them based on the professional requirements and beliefs. Following are the five types of ethical dilemmas:

— Confidentiality

— Role Conflict

— Counselor competence

— Conflicts with employer or institution

— Degree of dangerousness

American Counseling Association (ACA) based its first standards on the original American Psychological Associate code of ethics. ACA code of ethics was initiated by Donald Super and approved in 1961. Ethical Standards exist for many reasons. Without a code of established ethics, a group of people with similar interests can not be considered a professional organization. Helps professionalize an association on a general level but also provide some guidelines for the professional behaving of members.

Ethical standards protect the profession from government. Allow the profession to regulate itself and to function autonomously instead of being controlled by legislation and also help control internal disagreements and bickering. Ethical standards protect practitioners from the public especially malpractice suits.

Following are the Professional Codes of Ethics:

— Set of standards of conduct based upon as agreed on set of values.

— Code of ethics designed to offer formal statements for ensuring protection of clients.

— ACA standards are arranged under 8 major sectional headings:

1. Nature of Counseling Relationship
2. Confidentiality in counseling
3. Professional Competence
4. Relationships with other professionals
5. Evaluation assessment and interpretation
6. Teaching training and supervision
7. Research and publications
8. E thical considerations.

Ethically counselors must be aware of ethical codes and be able to differentiate an ethical dilemma from other types of dilemmas. Different ethical principles in a code that offer conflicting guidelines about what to do in a given situation. Conflicts may occur when counselors belong to 2 or more professional organizations where codes of ethics differ.

Treating individuals together as a system to overcome problems can use six values that affect counselors clients and the counseling process.

— Responsibility

— Integrity

— Commitment

— Freedom of Choice

— Empowerment

— Right to grieve

As recently as the 1960, counseling didn't have a strong enough identity as a profession to be recognized legally. Counselors legally recognized as professionals who provided personal, vocational and educational counseling. Counseling is the process through which a trained counselors assists an individual or group to make satisfactory and responsible decisions concerning personal, educational and career development.

Following are the four basic types of professional credentials

— *Inspection* - A state agency periodically examines the activities of a profession's practitioners to ascertain whether they are practicing the profession in a fashion consistent with public safety health and welfare.

— *Registration* - Requires submission of information to the state concerning the nature of their practice

— *Certification* - Person meets the minimum skills necessary to engage in that practice state board or department issues certificate to an individual in a specialty

— *Licensure* - Highest form of credentialing is licensure . Counselors experience trouble when laws are not clear and when conflict between the law and professional counseling ethics.

— *Confidentiality* - Ethical duty to fulfill a contract or promise clients that the information revealed during treatment will be protected from unauthorized disclosures.

— *Privacy* - Evolving legal concept that recognizes individuals rights to choose the time, circumstances and extent to which they wish to share or withhold personal information.

— *Privileged Communication* – Protects clients from having their confidential communication disclosed in court without permission.

Today, there are a number of apparent reasons that the counseling profession has failed to adequately address social and political issues. The first reason is that counseling theory and practice have continuously and steadfastly championed a model consistent with the socioeconomic and class distinctions of its practitioners and researchers. Second, counseling and psychology, particularly in the past two decades, have come to be part of the media marketplace of ideas.

Such counseling "ideas" are more likely to be presented in the form of fleeting images and 15-second sound bites than by a penetrating critical analysis of issues. Cliched and shallow pop psychology seems to best fit the media ideal of "therapeutic" solutions to devastating problems such as family violence. Third, it seems that counseling and psychology would rather analyze complex problems free of their historical and geographic contexts so as to maintain a "universal" claim for their strategies. But whatever the reason, the unwillingness to confront the many devastating contemporary social and political issues has occurred at a critical time when numerous community, school and social agencies in which counselors are employed are under attack from radical right-wing political and religious groups.

The ideology espoused by these groups indicts many counseling clients, who are victims of racial, sexual, political, and economic oppression, as entirely responsible for their own predicaments. The counseling profession's culpability and complicity in these attacks on clients has been its collective silence. Although some efforts have been made to raise gender, multicultural, and sexual issues, the debate has been severely curtailed by the profession's desire for increased legitimacy.

In America, the guidance and counseling movement was one of many humanitarian efforts that grew in response to the upheaval caused by the industrial revolution. The early guidance practitioners were public school teachers and administrators who used the disciplines of child study, psychometrics, and education to actuate laws. In fact, counseling was not even mentioned in the literature until 1931 and even after that there were still only a few full-time counselors before the 1950s. In the years after World War II, guidance and counseling underwent dramatic changes influenced by third-force psychology and humanism, which moved counseling away from the deterministic approaches of psychoanalysis and behaviorism toward theories that emphasized self-determination.

The formation of the American Personnel and Guidance Association in 1952 and the National Defense Education Act of 1958 had a significant impact on increasing the number of counseling professionals. Equally influential to the emerging counseling profession was the ongoing search for professional credibility. Guidance and counseling did not develop from a largely theoretical or philosophical base; rather, it borrowed its "frames of reference" from education, psychology, philosophy, and the physical sciences.

The responsiveness of counseling to political ends is severely curtailed. The exclusive adherence to a model of individual growth and change has resulted in the development of a professional organization and a role for the counselor that makes it extremely difficult for counselors to effectively address larger societal issues.

Counselors are mostly unaware of how their role has come to inhibit change. School counselors attempt to make intolerable schools tolerable for students; career counselors help clients make "realistic" career choices without examining underlying societal inequities or the nature of a market-driven economy that in many regions largely creates low-paying, temporary jobs.

Finally, many other counselors help the alienated client "adjust" to society without examining the source of that alienation in the culture. As mentioned, inherent in both the professional organization and the counselor's role are structural limitations that hinder both the organization's and the counselor's ability to work or advocate for societal change.

Several of the structural limitations built into the counselor's role have been articulated by many others over the years. There are several barriers to the rediscovery of counseling as a profession that can transform lives and society. First, the preoccupation of counseling and psychology with individualism and individual analysis of problems has served to depoliticize all social and interpersonal concerns. Second, as these professions struggle for public acceptance and credibility, they exhibit a growing tendency to support the dominant paradigm, rather than to advance change. Third, historically, counseling has adopted scientism as a model and made a claim of value neutrality.

This claim has created a barrier to the taking of a strong moral or principled stance. Fourth, as the profession continues to compete with similar professions for a share of resources and jobs, credentialing and accreditation have become a prominent issue among counselors.

The implementation of most counseling theory and practice continues to focus almost exclusively on the domain of the individual . Such a strategy for counseling seems to be aimed at changing the client's perception of reality rather than acknowledging that societal factors may be responsible for the client's plight. Cushman called this idea the "empty self." This concept of the empty self in modern counseling suggests that the self has come to stand apart from history and culture and is therefore apart from formative social and historical forces. The result has been a fragmented view of human development.

The concept of the autonomous self has been encapsulated and set apart from the outside. This inner world of changing moods, thoughts, and emotions has gained the helping professionals' stamp of reality. In the current language of counseling and human development theory, the individual is typically offered a "lifestyle solution". Instead of a dialogue anchored by a critical social analysis, the client is frequently told new coping skills, new insights based on awareness of internal subjective states, or corrective thinking strategies. Referring to family therapy, Imber-Black strongly suggested that unexamined, family therapy can easily contribute to the homeostatis of larger systems .... Understanding the ways that models emerge out of a given social and historical context, and how work... may be coopted by a broader and often hidden sociopolitical agenda can sensitize family therapists not only to the family but to themselves and their own context.

Power issues are seldom acknowledged-perhaps because counselors lack their own power base from "which to confront the basic values of institutions or the larger society". Power comes from the institutions in which counselors work and from the agencies that license them. It is granted contingent on one's working within prescribed boundaries that serve the larger system, and it can be taken away or certification denied if individuals attempt to use that power against those same institutions. Therefore, through training, preparation, and licensure practices, counselors frequently have come to adopt a core set of values that often stand in glaring contrast and contradiction to those held by many clients. Adoption of these values can constitute a form of cultural oppression when applied to minority group members, even if done unwittingly. They contended that such basic counseling values can "lend support to the belief that counseling is an egocentric part of the Establishment that interprets behavior exclusively from its own reference point". The socialization of counselors has been largely framed in the spirit of ethical neutrality.

The example of career counselors whose belief in pluralism, meritocracy, individualism, and pragmatism have provided the foundation of a belief system that upholds the notions of equal opportunity and free choice for everyone while "ignoring the way those choices are delimited by gender, race, and class socialization". It is this assumed position of value neutrality that has allowed counselors to portray themselves as professionally outside of the political ideologies that shape their current social thinking.

From this presumption of value neutrality counselors have made the claim of objectivity. Through such a claim of an objective science of helping, counselors have donned blinders, preventing themselves from viewing the social, political, and institutional nature of counseling theories and practices. It is this pretense to a position-free ideology that has provided the basic conceit of modern counseling practice and presented a formidable barrier to effective change in the discipline. Psychology has been a primary model from which the emphasis on individual assessment and diagnosis was borrowed.

In turn, psychology has imitated the medical-scientific model as the overarching paradigm by which to establish its own credibility. This reductionistic approach has underscored the intrapsychic focus and fostered increased specialization. Such specialization has debilitated the medical profession to the point at which a team of doctors are more likely now to address a client's symptomatology from the standpoint that the sum of a patient's symptoms equals the whole of a person.

This counseling-medical paradigm has been expressed in its many variations through community psychology, school counseling, college counseling, mental health counseling, and other social services and often amounts to little more than helping professionals serve as guardians or defenders of the status quo.

The outdated notion that the American Counseling Association (ACA) must be based on an objective and neutral scientific approach belies the fact that counselors make value judgments and choices every day that have political and social consequences for their clients. The guidance and counseling are sociopolitical processes in which neither theories nor techniques are value free.

Pressing political conditions that dramatically alter lives and affect the mental and emotional well-being of individuals has seldom been addressed. The short-term discussion and critical examination of salient political issues is blunted. Consequently, the search for the sociohistorical and political values inherent in research and practice has been put aside in favor of a discredited value-neutral approach. The dominant prescribed ideology, masquerading as apolitical and therefore "scientific," can continue to frame what are or are not acceptable and appropriate research and practice concerns.

In more recent years, the quest for legitimacy through imitation has led the counseling profession into the domain of other health professionals, with the result that organizations of those professions have made efforts to restrict that movement. The damaging nature of this polarization among helping professionals has divided all of the power and set one against the other. These turf wars are many; witness the frequency with which the following tend to occur: counselors' fight with the marriage and family therapists for territory, social workers pitted against elementary school counselors for jobs, and psychologists battling against psychiatrists for the ability to prescribe medication.

Counselors have created their own system of credentialing and now seek to license counselors in every state and accredit counselor training programs. Aubrey's prophetic words have heralded the final regression to the mean during the summer of 1992 as the acronym for the organization was reduced to three letters (ACA), placing it symbolically beside the AMA (American Medical Association), and both APAs (American Psychological Association, and American Psychiatric Association).

Yet, it will do little to change the stepchild status of counseling vis-a-vis these other three organizations unless insurance companies replace the National Registry with the Yellow Pages as a hierarchical guide to mental health services.

Evidence of a major paradigmatic shift has been presented to the profession in the form of social constructionism and narrative-based approaches to the social sciences. Constructivists' relationships and their narrative description have served as a central and vital means by which meaning is determined for individuals and communities of individuals. Such a postmodern approach to identity and reality emerges from meaningful, horizontal relationships free of constraining preestablished "standards."

The participants in the narrative dialogue need to be free to construct new meanings for identity and fruitful action. At this point, taking action is the result of relational self-favoring interdependence, context specificity, and ongoing dialogue over the traditional values placed on detached rationality and the self-contained, autonomous self. Participants in the dialogue, whether they be counselor and client, teacher and parent, or counselor and administrator, are free to "construct" a dialogue in which the relational aspects of environments are emphasized.

As counselors become more socially and politically aware, environmental causes of human problems come to take center stage. We can now no longer draw artificial distinctions between the outside world of events and inner, subjective perceptions. Taken a step further, political awareness makes it difficult to distinguish individual well-being from collective well-being. The counselors can educate themselves regarding macro issues. This requires interdisciplinary academic perspectives in which students encounter coursework and experience in such disciplines as political science, economics, history, and anthropology.

The counseling professionals need to expand the context through an understanding that all human thought and action is context dependent. When counselors have begun these steps, they need to deal with the resistance that they will encounter in their academic discipline and professional organizations. In addition, counselors ought to have the courage to publicly confront elected officials who pander to the baser instincts of the citizens by using race, sex, and class to pit one segment of society against others for their personal political gain.

Bibliography

Holland, J.L. (1973), *Making Vocational Choices: a Theory of Careers,* Prentice-Hall, Englewood Cliffs, NJ.

Jackson, C. (1993), *The case for diversity in computer-aided careers guidance systems: a response to Watts,* British Journal of Guidance and Counselling, Vol.21 No.2, pp.189-195.

Lee, C. (2000), *Cybercounseling and empowerment: bridging the digital divide,* in Bloom, J.W. & Walz, G.R. (eds.)

McKinlay, B. (1989), *Information systems in career development: history and prospects.*

Offer, M. & Sampson, J.P. (1999), *Quality in the content and use of information and communications technology in guidance,* British Journal of Guidance and Counselling, Vol.27 No.4, pp.501-516.

Offer, M. (1998), *Guidance' websites: we're here, because we're here, because we're here?,* Newscheck, Vol.9 No.4, pp.13-14.

Offer, M., Sampson, J.P. & Watts, A.G. (2001), *Technology and the Future: Strategic Implications for Higher Education Careers Services of Technically Mediated Service Delivery,* Higher Education Careers Services Unit, Manchester (in press).

Oliver, L.W. & Zack, J.S. (1999), *Career assessment on the Internet: an exploratory study,* Journal of Career Assessment, Vol.7 No.4, pp.323-356.

Organisation for Economic Co-operation and Development (2000), *Learning to Bridge the Digital Divide,* OECD, Paris.

Sampson, J.P. (1999a), *Integrating Internet-based distance guidance with services provided in career centers,* Career Development Quarterly, Vol.47 No.3, pp.243-254.

Sampson, J.P. (1999b), *Effective design and use of Internet-based career resources and services: a North American perspective,* paper to International Association for Educational and Vocational Guidance conference, Wellington, New Zealand (mimeo).

Sampson, J.P., Palmer, M. & Watts, A.G. (1999b), *Who Needs Guidance?, Centre for Guidance Studies,* University of Derby.

Sampson, J.P., Peterson, G.W., Reardon, R.C. & Lenz, J.G. (1999a), *Improving Career Services through Readiness Assessment: a Cognitive Information Processing Approach,* Center for the Study of Technology in Counseling and Career Development, Florida State University, Tallahassee, FL (mimeo).

Tait, A. (1999), *Face-to-face and at a distance: the mediation of guidance and counselling through the new technologies,* British Journal of Guidance and Counselling, Vol. 27 No.1, pp.113-122.

Watts, A.G. & Dent, G. (2002), *Let your fingers do the walking': the use of telephone helplines in career information and guidance,* British Journal of Guidance and Counselling, Vol.30 No.1 (in press).

Watts, A.G. (1986), *The role of the computer in careers guidance,* International Journal for the Advancement of Counselling, Vol.9 No.2, pp.145-158.

Watts, A.G. (1993), *The politics and economics of computer-aided careers guidance systems,* British Journal of Guidance and Counselling, Vol.21 No.2, pp.175-188.

Watts, A.G. (1996a), *Computers in guidance,* in Watts, A.G., Law, B., Killeen, J., Kidd, J.M. & Hawthorn, R., Rethinking Careers Education and Guidance: Theory, Policy and Practice, pp. 269- 283, Routledge, London.

Watts, A.G. (1996b), *Careers guidance and public policy,* in Watts, A.G., Law, B., Killeen, J., Kidd, J.M. & Hawthorn, R., Rethinking Careers Education and Guidance: Theory, Policy and Practice, pp. 380-391, Routledge, London.

Watts, A.G. (2001), *Second International Symposium on Career Development and Public Policy: rapporteur's report,* Canadian Career Development Foundation, Ottawa (mimeo).

Index